The Gospel According to John

By Mrs. T. M. Constance

Book 3 - Lessons 21-30

We believe the Bible is God's Word, a divine revelation, in the original language
verbally inspired in its entirety, and that it is the supreme infallible authority
in all matters of faith and conduct.
(II Peter 1:21; II Timothy 3:16)

Printed in the United States of America

Published by Explorer's Bible Study
2652 Hwy. 46 South
P.O. Box 425
Dickson, TN 37056-0425
1-615-446-7316

Jesus Gives a New Commandment and Announces His Departure
John 13:31-38; John 14:1-14

I. Jesus Glorified
(John 13:31-32)

When Judas left the room where Jesus and the disciples had observed the last supper, Jesus knew his purpose was to reveal to the rulers, the enemies of Jesus, where He would be and how they might seize Him. Jesus saw Himself and the Father glorified through all that was to transpire in the coming hours. Jesus said, *"Now the Son of Man is glorified, and God is glorified in Him."* The title, *"Son of Man,"* expresses His incarnation and redemptive work. As the Son of Man, that purpose for which He came into the world would be accomplished and He would be glorified. *"And God is glorified in Him."* The glorification of Jesus is always the glorification of God because God was in Christ reconciling the world unto Himself. God's love, truth and righteousness sent Jesus into the world for our redemption, and this necessitated the suffering and the cross. *"And glorify Him immediately."* in all probability carries the meaning of victory over death and the grave in the resurrection and ascension of Jesus Christ.

II. The New Commandment
(John 13:33-35)
A. The Lord's Departure
(John 13:33)

Knowing that in a few hours the daily association with His disciples would come to an end, Jesus addresses them most affectionately as *"little children."* Jesus wants them to be sure of His tender concern for them. They would not be able to go with Him. Jesus had to face the cross alone, but Jesus also told Peter that afterward they would follow Him.

B. New Commandment: "Love One Another" (John 13:34-35)

When His presence would be taken from them they would still have one another, and Jesus admonished them to love each other as He had loved them. The content of the commandment is very simple: *"that you love one another."* Where love exists, it is bound to show itself and to affect others. This love Jesus commanded embraced all who through faith in Him had united. It is a love new in its very nature. Jesus brought into the world and testified to His own a love that was different — a love for and in Christ, reaching out to others.

III. Christ's Warning to Peter
(John 13:36-38)

It seems that Peter was not satisfied to give up His Lord and to concentrate his love on his fellow disciples. He was determined to cling to His Master regardless of the words of Christ. Involved in Peter's question was a deep love for His Lord. His love could not endure the thought of being separated from Him. Jesus understood the purpose of Peter's question and said, *"you cannot follow Me now."* Temporary separation was inevitable. Peter was not yet prepared or ready for the place where Jesus was going. He misjudged his own moral strength and declared he was ready to lay down his life for his Master. Knowing Peter better than he knew himself, Jesus warned him that before the crowing of the cock Peter would have denied Him three times. This prediction of his denial seems to have had a profound effect on Peter, and he does not speak again until the end of the discourses. His readiness to die for Jesus was not quite what he thought it was. It was Jesus who needed to die for Peter. The word of Jesus to Peter was with special purpose for this disciple; it would be the means of bringing Peter to repentance. When he heard the cock crowing, the words of Jesus came to his mind, and this together with the look Jesus gave him caused Peter to go out and weep bitterly in repentance. Peter had a deep love for Jesus but needed to learn the place of submission and humility. Peter, presumptuous, self-confident and proud, had yet to learn to yield his weaknesses to God, who was able to change Peter from being self-confident to placing his confidence in God. Peter was special to Jesus, and Jesus knew what Peter would become. According to tradition, Peter also was crucified because he chose to follow Jesus all the way.

IV. Jesus Christ: The Way, Truth and Life (John 14:1-14)

A. Jesus Comforts His Disciples (John 14:1-4)

John 14 is a continuation of the previous chapter. Jesus and His disciples were in the upper room where they had eaten together. Judas had left as Jesus suggested he do to finish quickly the plans he had already begun for betraying his Master. With the warning given Peter, the little gathering had reason to be troubled. Jesus had told them of His leaving them and that they would not be able to be with Him. This was shattering to men who had left all to follow Him. Jesus knew that within a very short time there would be reason for even greater distress. Amidst this, He told them not to be troubled and issued a call for them to have faith. As they believed in God, they must also have faith and believe in Jesus in whom God was perfecting His perfect will and purpose for their salvation and for the sins of the world. It seems that Jesus looked beyond the few hours of suffering and death to that which should bring comfort and hope of a place in heaven being prepared for them by their Master. The consequences would be that if Jesus left them for this purpose, He would return. This has reference to the second advent of the Lord Jesus Christ. Nothing is said about the nature of the place Christ prepares for us, but it is enough to know we will be with Him. When we think of heaven, it is with all the tenderness and attractiveness, the restfulness and the happiness that lie in the word "home." The mansions are a reality, in actual existence. God has provided them and Jesus assures us of it. The mansions are many, and the promise to the disciples is that they,

too, shall enter these mansions. Jesus said, *"I will come again and receive you to myself."* Jesus demands abiding trust and faith in God and in Himself, even though much appears to be a mystery. Christ going away to the Father's house had as its purpose a reunion. Apart from Christ's death and the work of the Holy Spirit, there would have been no place in heaven for the disciples. Jesus, being separated from His disciples for a little while, would be the means of bringing them joy, the very opposite of trouble and distress.

Jesus told the disciples where He was going and what that would mean to them, and then He added another word of assurance, *"And where I go you know, and the way you know."* Jesus had been teaching the disciples how to follow Him, and if they followed Him they would know the way.

V. Jesus Answers Thomas' Question (John 14:5-7)

A. Thomas' Question (John 14:5)

"Thomas said to Him, 'Lord, we do not know where You are going, and how can we know the way?'" It seems that Thomas was speaking for all the disciples, taking for granted that they all felt the same way he did. Thomas actually contradicts Jesus and tells Him that they do not know the way as He has assumed. This was really not the contradiction of unbelief, but of discouraged faith. Thomas was really searching for knowledge and needed to know exactly what Jesus meant by saying that they knew the way, and this is why there was no rebuke in Jesus' answer to Thomas.

B. Jesus' Answer (John 14:6)

The question of Thomas gives occasion to the great declaration of Jesus when He said, *"I am the way, the truth, and the life. No one comes to the Father except through Me."* This is the sixth of the seven great "I am's" of the Gospel of John. Jesus does not just show us the way, but He is the way. He not only teaches us and guides us in the way, but He has given to us a new and living way and this is possible only because He is the way. He is the only way to God. He is the only true way. He is the way in every act, word and attitude and is the only mediator between God and man.

"I am the Way." Not I am the principle by which you may come. We are not saved by a principle no matter how good that principle may be, but by a person - Jesus Christ. The emphasis is on Jesus, the Word that became flesh and dwelt among us, full of grace and truth. He is the way to God the Father; He is the way to heaven. This is not a lifeless road that one travels in his own strength, but one that through faith in Jesus Christ carries us to our destination. It is only through faith in Him alone, by entrusting ourselves completely to Him, by forsaking all other ways for reaching God and heaven. Apart from Jesus Christ, there is no salvation from sin and no way to God or heaven.

"I am the Truth." Truth follows *"the way"* and then there is life. Jesus is the actual embodiment of truth. He is the very reality of all God's grace toward sinners, of all God's plans of grace and their execution, of all God's gifts of grace in those plans. As a human mediator, Moses could give the law, but grace and truth came through the living person of Jesus Christ. It is for us to know and to trust Jesus Christ in one inward spiritual act as *"the truth."* Just as the way is a living way, so also the truth is a living truth. It influences our whole life. It sets us free. Not basically "it" but *"He"* is the truth.

"I am the Life." Jesus is the light of life, the source and giver of life. Death means separation from God, but life means communion with the Father. Jesus Christ is the way because He is the truth and the life. "Truth" is the complete reliability of Jesus in all He does and is. The only life worthy of His name is that which Jesus gives, for He is life itself. On the evening before His crucifixion, Jesus is asserting the uniqueness and the sufficiency of His mission for the salvation of all who come to Him. One who would soon be hanging on a cross and by means of the false accusations by wicked men, and One whose body was soon to be laid in a tomb, said, *"I am the way, the truth and the life."*

The disciples, although they had known Jesus, had left their homes and given up all to follow Him, did not know Him in His full significance. To know Jesus is to know the Father. John 1:18 says, *"No one has seen God at any time. The only begotten Son, who is in the bosom of the Father, He has declared Him."* *"And from now on"* designates the great new period beginning with the events of this night and extending to all the great experiences of the future. The Father would give His Son unto death, would raise Him again from the dead, and would seat Him at His right hand. Jesus would send the Holy Spirit into the world to give power to His followers. They would know the Father as never before. The final days of their experience with Jesus would crown all that Jesus had done previously.

VI. Jesus and Philip (John 14:8-12)

A. The Father and the Son

"Lord, show us the Father, and it is sufficient for us." Philip was one of the first disciples Jesus called to follow Him. His name is Greek and he came from Bethsaida in Galilee. He brought Nathaniel to Jesus. The request he made to Jesus shows a human longing for a tangible God. He was asking for a visible manifestation of the Father's glory. Obviously Philip had failed to listen to what Jesus told Thomas, and Jesus gave him a gentle rebuke. Philip seemed to lack a comprehension of what the mission of Jesus really was in what the Father had sent Him to do. Philip wanted to see the Father with his physical eyes, little realizing that this would profit him nothing. To the unbelieving Jews, Jesus had answered when they asked the question, "Where is thy Father?" He replied that if they had known Him, they would have known the Father also. How could Philip ask such a question? He had been a follower of Jesus for three years; his question was certainly not in harmony with his faith. In order to make clear to the disciples and to correct any doubt or misconception in their minds, Jesus again points to the constant evidence and manifestation of this oneness He had with the Father. Jesus was dealing with a faith that at the moment did not see clearly. The words and works of Jesus both proceed from the Father. They serve to confirm faith, to strengthen it and make it strong. Jesus dealt with the disciples as believers, and the grounds for their belief should have been that Jesus is in the Father and the Father in Him. Whoever hears and sees Jesus' works sees the Father Himself in words and works. The words and works of Jesus should be all-sufficient for them to continue in the faith. Works establish the words and the words establish the works. The disciples are admonished to take Jesus at His word. This is the highest form of faith. But if this is difficult, let them believe because of the works.

Daily Bible Study Questions for Group Discussion

Note: Read notes and scripture references before answering the questions. Some questions are for those more advanced in Bible study. Try to answer all questions but don't be discouraged if some seem a little hard. Unless otherwise instructed, use Bible only in answering questions.

FIRST DAY: Read notes on Lesson #21; read I Corinthians 10:12.

1. How does Peter's self-confidence in **John 13:37-38** enforce Paul's warning in **I Corinthians 10:12**?

2. On this rather bleak night before Jesus was to leave His disciples for a while, what phrase do you think would be of the most comfort to them from the first few verses?

3. From **John 14:4-11**, what claims did Jesus make for Himself:
    (a) regarding man's approach to God?

    (b) in regard to man's knowledge of God?

    (c) in regard to the source and origin of His words and works?

4. As a consequence of Jesus' return to His Father, what prospect did Jesus set before His disciples?

SECOND DAY: Read John 14:12-31.

5. What are the two promises Jesus gives His disciples in **John 14:12-14**?

6. After Jesus assured His disciples He was not deserting them, He admonished them to loyalty, devotion and action. What verse would necessitate a personal choice on the part of each disciple?

7. Jesus speaks of the three persons of the Godhead in **John 14:16**. What phrase refers to Jesus? What phrase refers to the Holy Spirit?

THIRD DAY: Read John 14:17-26.

8. What words or phrases describe the relationship that the Holy Spirit would have to the disciples?

9. What five things will happen in the experience of the disciples when the Spirit comes?

10. What is the necessary condition on the part of the disciples before they can experience what Christ has promised them?

11. If Jesus were going away, He would not be with the disciples to teach them. It would be difficult for the disciples to remember all that Jesus taught them. What promise did He give to them that would assure them help in the blessing of memory?

12. This may be difficult, but referring to the previous question, what does this imply?

FOURTH DAY: Continue Reading John 14:17-26.

13. Do you think that the question Judas asked in **John 14:22** was based on the idea some of the Jews had that Jesus would manifest Himself in power to the world in restoring and setting up His kingdom at this time?

14. (a) What two types of people are mentioned in **John 14:23-24**?

    (b) What were the results after the criteria had been examined?

15. What are some of the contrasts Jesus makes between the world and the disciples?

FIFTH AND SIXTH DAYS: Read John 14:27-31.

16. How many things do we learn about "peace" in **John 14:27**?

17. Think about **John 14:28**. What do you think Jesus is really saying to His disciples?

18. In **verses 30 and 31**, what do you learn about: Satan? The Father? Christ? the World?

19. What admonition given by Christ to His disciples can we apply in our own life situations?

20. What spiritual applications can we make regarding love and obedience to Christ?

21. According to **John 14:26**, what responsibility does this place on us as to our study of the Word of God?

Notes

The Promise of the Holy Spirit
John 14:12-31

I. Jesus' Promise of Greater Works (John 14:12-14)

A. Jesus Stresses Personal Commitment (John 14:12)

"He who believes in Me, the works that I do he will do also; and greater works than these he will do." Believing what Jesus says, believing in the person of Jesus as the way, the truth and the life, One in essence with the Father, the Mediator and the Redeemer — to you who have truly identified with Jesus Christ and continue in this faith, this promise is made. Faith in Christ is an unquestionable certainty.

B. The "Greater Works" (John 14:12)

Jesus made three claims regarding His oneness with the Father: two in the previous verses and one in the verse under consideration. Evidence of His miracles; evidence of His words or testimony; and now Jesus promises to His followers a third evidence, that of a new spiritual life empowered by the Holy Spirit. In this Christ said that we, as His followers, would experience *"greater works."* We need to read this correctly. Jesus did not say that we would do "greater miracles." Even the miracles of Christ, great as they were and beneficent as they were, were confined to the body and did not directly touch the spirit of man. Christ wrought His miracles that men, beginning with what they could see and appreciate, might be led to believe in and trust Him. Now He is telling His disciples that these works which He had been doing would be exceeded by the greatest of miracles, that of reaching the souls of men with the message of salvation through Christ. This work would not be deleted by disease and death, but would be permanent. This greater work would not be confined to Palestine, but should be preached to the whole world.

C. Conditional Circumstances for the Promise

"Because I go to My Father." By going to His Father the work of Christ would not be stopped, but would be continued by His disciples. It is the death and resurrection of Christ that brought salvation to the hearts of men, and this message must be preached to a lost and dying world. Sinners converted to Jesus Christ by God's grace carry the gospel to the ends of the earth where souls are saved for eternity. The greater works is the account of the Acts of the Apostles, men and women filled with the Holy Spirit preaching the redeeming love of Christ. Without the exaltation of Jesus, the promise could not be fulfilled. After His death on the cross, Jesus returned to His Father as one having completed His mission. With redemption accomplished, the greater works of the gospel of redemption begin. The disciples would be instruments through whom God would work.

D. The Importance of Prayer (John 14:13-14)

1. In Christ's Name

Whatever the disciples ask *"in My name, that I will do."* This does not mean by "My authority" or in "My stead." It does not mean simply using the name of Jesus as a formula. Prayer must be in accordance with all that name represents. The revelation by which we know Jesus is found in the text John 1:12) *"But as many as received Him, to them He gave the right to become children of God, to those who believe in His name."* This covers the person as well as the work of Christ. It involves faith in all Christ stands for. There are many titles for Christ, and it takes in all of them as well as their meanings.

2. The Object of Our Prayer

To pray in the name of Jesus implies that the prayer is directed to the Father. The purpose is that the Father may be glorified *"in the Son."* The two are inseparable. The Father and the Son are so intimately related that what one does the other does also. Jesus said, *"that I will do."* That which you ask in prayer, believing, I will answer. Thus the work of Christ continues as He is in heaven with His Father. Jesus Christ is the Mediator; the Father answers through Him; He will do what He promised.

3. The Hearer of Prayer

In verses 12, 13 and 14 we are told what the believer will do and then what Jesus will do. We know that He hears and answers prayer because He said he would. This we must believe. Sometimes our wavering faith wonders how and when, but God fulfills every promise to us as His children. Sometimes His answer is "Yes," sometimes "No," and sometimes "Wait." Because God sees the end from the beginning, He knows best how to answer our petitions.

In His work, our doing is dependent on Him, and the believer *"will do"* the promised works. What Jesus does depends on Himself and His own will, and He will do what He promised so that the Father may be glorified. *"If you ask anything in My name, I will do it."* The implication of this text is that it is no longer what the disciples ask, but on the person who answers. What Jesus wants to say is that prayer may be directed to Him as well as to the Father. When we pray to Jesus, the petitions are still *"in My name"* and include His relation to the Father. Again, Jesus Christ and His Father are equal and their will is one. Jesus gave the disciples this comfort before He left them. What a blessed assurance: greater works and answers to prayer!

E. Loving Obedience to Christ's Commands (John 14:15)

For the promised works and answers to prayer, there must be faith on the part of the disciples. Following this, Jesus gives the promise of the Holy Spirit, and this includes the fruit of faith. Both are subjective conditions: *"He who believes in Me"* and *"if you love Me."* There is no love without the presence of faith, and one who does not trust cannot love. Jesus is speaking to believers, and He expects their love

and evidence of that love to be expressed in guarding His precepts in contending for the teachings of Jesus. Being obedient to the teaching of Christ must not be treated carelessly. This includes all believers.

II. Jesus Teaches the Disciples about the Holy Spirit (John 14:16-26)

A. Jesus' Promise of the Comforter (John 14:16)

Jesus said He would pray to His Father, and the effect of that prayer would be that the Father would give the disciples another Comforter. Jesus would be leaving, and they would not have the same companionship as they have had in His earthly ministry. But they would not be left alone in their conflict with the world. In addition to the promise of the *"Comforter,"* this One who would be a gift from God, the disciples are assured that He would be with them forever. He would not leave them as Jesus must, but would be an abiding presence eternally.

Jesus said, *"And I will pray the Father, and He will give."* These are reciprocal acts. The Holy Spirit is a gift from the Father as Jesus Christ is a gift from the Father. The Holy Spirit as the Comforter takes the place of Jesus at the side of the disciples. In John 14:26, He brings things to their remembrance. In John 15:26, He testifies to the disciples concerning Jesus. In John 16:7, Jesus sends the Holy Spirit to His disciples. In John 16:14 the Holy Spirit shall glorify Jesus, taking what is His and showing it unto them. In John 14:16 and John 16:7, the disciples do not call the Comforter to them; the Father and Jesus give and send the Holy Spirit to the disciples.

B. The Holy Spirit - the "Spirit of Truth" (John 14:17)

Jesus Christ is truth. The teaching of the Spirit in this text is contrasted with that of the Word. Teaching by means of the Word apart from the Spirit of truth can leave us with a confused idea of the divine. All it does is leave an image of the truth. The teaching of the Spirit causes the divine truth to enter our hearts. It makes the Word truth for us; it gives to it a reality within us. It is not difficult to understand why the world cannot receive the Spirit of truth. It is in opposition to truth. The world is blinded by the devil's delusion and has false and foolish explanations for the Spirit's manifestations. They lack an experiential knowledge of Jesus Christ and the Holy Spirit, who speaks in the Word. They do not know the power of God nor the saving grace of Jesus Christ; therefore the Holy Spirit is foreign to them. They reject the conviction of the Holy Spirit upon their hearts and harden themselves to that which is spiritual. Faith, love and obedience delight in God and His Word. Its promises and comfort are indications of the Spirit's presence in us and of our knowledge of who He really is. Jesus said to the disciples, *"but you know Him, for He dwells with you and will be in you."* The day of Pentecost was to come following the ascension of Jesus to heaven. Following that day, the Holy Spirit would be within them. The experience would be that of new dynamic power to effect the work of Christ in a hostile world. We must ever keep in mind, however, that the Holy Spirit is not just a power or an influence in our lives. The Holy Spirit is a person, the third person of the Trinity and works in unity with the Father and Son.

C. Jesus Reaffirms His Love and Concern for the Disciples (John 14:18-21)

The crucifixion was very near. After Jesus' death the world would see Him no more. He would be removed from them physically because they rejected Him. It will be different with the disciples. They would be separated from their Master, but only for a little while. After His death Christ lived and His living had implications for them. His resurrection guarantees that they will live also. When Christ was risen from the grave and the Holy Spirit was given at Pentecost, the disciples knew the truth of Christ's relationship with the Father, and they knew He dwelt in them and they in Him.

We can have an intellectual concept of Christ and of His commandments. This is one thing, but to love Christ and keep His commandments is another. We are to observe His teachings daily. Obedience is an indication of true love. The one who truly loves Christ will be loved of the Father.

D. Judas Questions the Manifestation of Christ (John 14:22)

This Judas is generally identified with Thaddeus. He was concerned that Jesus was not to manifest Himself to the world but only to a select few. Jesus

had talked about being the Saviour of the world and that He had many other sheep and that His mission was to all men. This chapter imparts to us something we all need to learn, and that is to bring our problems, theological and otherwise, to the Lord. Thomas, Philip and Judas all had questions that they brought to Christ. They needed answers, and to know they could go to the One who could give them an answer to their doubts and difficulties. Today we have the Word of God and the Holy Spirit, which should be our source of spiritual knowledge. We are instructed that if we lack wisdom we are to ask of God, and this means by prayer, seeking answers for the perplexities of life. There are none too great and none too small but what God is not interested. He is concerned about everything that touches our lives.

Judas, being acquainted with only the bodily manifestation of Jesus, wondered how Christ could show Himself to His own and the world not see Him; also why Christ would make that difference.

E. Jesus' Answer to Judas' Question (John 14:23-24)

While Jesus seemed to avoid an answer to the question Judas asked and to just continue on with His discourse, He really answered the point raised by Judas. He repeated His teaching concerning their duty, asserting that love to Him would cause men to keep His word and obey it. He repeated and enlarged on what he had already said to encourage them, assuring them that the Father and He would love such, and that His manifestation of Himself would be by His coming to be with them and abiding with them. There is a contrast drawn by Jesus to the one who loves Him and keeps His word and others who do not love Him and disregard His word, which is evidence of lack of love for Him. It seems that in response to the question, Jesus focuses attention on individual and personal responsibility. To love or not to love is a choice. We can be so concerned about the deeper counsel of God that we neglect our personal walk with Him. There are privileges and blessings in being a child of God, but there are also great responsibilities in reaching out to the world by word and example of true Christian living. In all of Christ's tender love, His sovereignty is not laid aside. He still insists on the necessity of love and obedience for the fulfillment of His promises. Christ will never make void what He has promised for the encouragement of His children. The one who loves Him will find himself enriched in both the love of the Father and the Son. It is good to remember that obedience to the Word of God is not required as a simple act of love and courtesy, but as a testimony of subjection to divine authority. We seemingly would prefer to bypass such teaching today and do our own thing, set our own rules, and be governed by them rather than God's Word.

III. The Conclusion of Jesus' Discourse with His Disciples (John 14:25-31)

A. Benefit of the Holy Spirit in Teaching (John 14:25-26)

Although Christ had taught the disciples many things, He knew in the little time He had with them that He would not be able to teach them all they needed to know. What He did teach them while He was with them they would not be able to understand or retain. He affirms the promise of the Holy Spirit, whom the Father would send in Christ's name, who would teach them all things and bring all things to their remembrance whatever He had taught them. The Holy Spirit will not teach anything contrary to what Christ has already taught. After His resurrection, Christ continued with His disciples for forty days, instructing them and *"speaking of the things pertaining to the kingdom of God"* (Acts 1:3). Jesus wanted the disciples to understand how they would be blessed by the presence and work of this divine person, the Holy Spirit.

We have the promise, *"And bring to your remembrance all things that I said to you."* in the writings of the four gospels. The Holy Spirit enabled them to recall every utterance of Jesus in its true meaning. It is every believer's privilege to also trust that the Holy Spirit will bring to our remembrance the things we have learned and which are needful in our ministry to others, a word fitly spoken and applied by the Holy Spirit to meet the need in our life as well as in the lives of others.

B. Jesus Leaves a Legacy and a Treasure (John 14:27-31)

"Peace I leave with you, My peace I give to you; not as the world gives do I give to you. Let not your heart be troubled, neither let it be afraid." This is the last part of the discourse Jesus gave to His disciples, and He ends it with words of consolation and encouragement. True peace is Christ's peace, and will be continued after He leaves His disciples. It is not dependent upon His bodily presence. Christ's peace is far different than that which the world gives, which is freedom from outward trouble when there is inward turmoil. The world wishes peace when they cannot give it, but the peace Jesus gives is real and effectual. It is only in Him that we can experience the kind of peace that will deliver us from trouble and fear.

In the last verses of this chapter we have a summary of what Jesus taught the disciples concerning His departure and return to them. Jesus admonished them to rejoice rather than to be sad and fearful. His exaltation out of this time of humiliation into glory with the Father should have made them rejoice, as this exaltation would mean many advantages to them also. Christ was not only leaving them but would also return, which should have been a deterrent to their grief. It is good for a Christian to examine his love for Jesus Christ. There is a danger sometimes of what may be troubled hearts, and fear may in reality be self-love rather than a love for Jesus Christ. True, the disciples were going to be separated from their Master for a time, and there could have been that element of self-pity and self-love in that they did not share with Christ the joy of His return to His Father.

"That you may believe" are Christ's words to the disciples. He had taken much time to train and teach them that they might believe. Christ, by His exaltation, gives such proof of His deity and fullness, and this would place even a greater responsibility on His people for believing. The evidence would be great and complete through Christ's death, resurrection and ascension.

Christ was about to leave them to be subjected to Satan's malice. The disciples must not allow themselves to be overtaken with fear and trouble, but to remain faithful. Jesus Christ went forth to die out of love for a lost world and in obedience to His Father. Christ was willing to do this, and He said to His disciples, *"Arise, let us go from here."* Christ voluntarily yielded Himself for the redemption of sinners and He did this *"But that the world may know that I love the Father, and as the Father gave Me commandment, so I do."*

Daily Bible Study Questions for Group Discussion

Note: Read notes and scripture references before answering the questions. Some questions are for more advanced in Bible study. Try to answer all questions but don't be discouraged if some seem a little hard. Unless otherwise instructed, use Bible only in answering questions.

FIRST DAY: Read notes on Lesson #22.

1. From the scripture text and the notes, what did you find most helpful regarding the teaching on the Holy Spirit?

2. Two solutions are given in **John 14** as a deterrent to troubled and fearful hearts. What are they?

3. What are some of the contrasts in this week's lesson between the world and the believer?

4. What are two words that would best sum up **John 14** as far as a positive personal commitment to Christ?

SECOND DAY: Read John 15:1-17.

5. What two kinds of branches are mentioned in the first verses of **John 15**?

6. Jesus said that His Father was the husbandman of this true vine. What action does He take concerning the character of the two branches?

7. What one word is used that expresses the important relationship of the vine and the branches? How many times is this word used in the first ten verses of **John 15**?

8. Who is the vine? Who is the husbandman? Who are the branches?

9. Thinking of the twelve disciples Jesus had chosen, which one would be considered an unfruitful branch and at this time had been removed? Explain why.

THIRD DAY:

10. What is the real purpose of the vine? What is the result if a branch does not fulfill its purpose?

11. What is the five-stage result of an unfruitful branch?

12. Besides Judas in the New Testament, can you think of an Old Testament character who would have fit the description of one who by deliberate choice would come under the same judgment as here described?

13. What characteristics of one abiding in Christ are found in the **first ten verses** of **John 15**?

FOURTH DAY:

14. What illustration did Jesus use that should motivate the Christian to greater love and devotion in his service to Christ?

15. What does the love of Christ include for us?

16. What is the purpose or results of our abiding in Christ?

FIFTH AND SIXTH DAYS:

17. What would demonstrate the disciples love for Jesus?

18. What new identity did Jesus give His disciples and what was His reason for doing this?

19. Friends generally choose each other. What is different about the friendship of Jesus and His disciples that is given in a negative and an affirmative statement?

20. What ingredient is important in our work for Christ and as Jesus admonished His disciples to do, that work for Him might be fruitful?

Notes

The True Vine
John 15:1-16

Introduction

Jesus uses the illustration of the vine and the branches to teach the importance of fruitfulness in the Christian life. This is not the result of human achievement, but of abiding in Christ who is the true vine. Jesus outlines this difficult but important way of service. Branches that are not fruitful are purged. This was the last opportunity Jesus would have to warn His disciples about the consequences of faithlessness. Judas was one who chose not to remain with Jesus but rather to manifest the work of Satan. Jesus had been talking to the disciples about the Holy Spirit, and through the work of the Holy Spirit in their lives, they would be fruitful. The symbolism Jesus used would be understood by the disciples. In the Old Testament, Israel is described as the Lord's vineyard. It was natural that the Israelite, acquainted with the Old Testament, would associate fruitfulness, both natural and spiritual, with the idea of a vine (Psalm 80:8, 14; 128:3; Isaiah 5:1-7; Ezekiel 17:8; Joel 2:22; Zechariah 8:12; Malachi 3:11). The fact that at times the vine failed to bring forth desirable fruit was also known. The application to spiritual fruit-bearing is found in Isaiah 5:4 and Jeremiah 2:21.

I. Abiding in Jesus as Branches in the Vine

A. The Identity of the True Vine (John 15:1)

"I am the true vine, and My Father is the vinedresser." The text does not give us information as to where Jesus uttered these words in teaching the disciples. The last verse in John 14 says, *"Arise, let us go from here."* It is possible that He continued to talk to them before they left the Upper Room. It may have been as He and His disciples walked slowly by the temple and on to the Garden. Jesus was always a great teacher, and uppermost in His mind were the concerns of His pupils. His time in terms of years was comparatively short; now it was only a matter of hours and there was so much to say. Jesus knew that had He taught it sooner, the disciples would not have grasped the full meaning of His words.

Jesus used the symbol of the vine because He wanted to represent the permanent spiritual union of His disciples with Himself; therefore a perennial, and not an annual plant must be selected. The vine represented well the fruitfulness of Christ and believers, thus necessitating a cultivated plant that yielded fruit on every branch. It represents Christ, too, in that He was dependent on His Father who was the husband-man. Other trees stand alone, but the vine is dependent on a source for support. Jesus embodied the complete will and purpose of the Father. Jesus did not say He was like the vine; He said, *"I am the vine."* The point of comparison between Christ and the vine is the organic union by which the life of the trunk becomes that of the branches. Jesus wanted the disciples to appreciate the value of this plant which God Himself has planted, and will therefore care for it. The Father and the Son are never regarded as separate, but as working together as One.

B. The Vine and the Branches Go Together (John 15:2)

God the Father watches over the vine to secure fruitfulness. Every fruitless branch He takes away. Branches need much care in order that they may bear fruit. There are two kinds of branches: the fruitful and the unfruitful. There are two alternatives: remaining in Christ in order to produce as much fruit as possible, or separation from Him in judgment. Jesus wanted His disciples to know He would dwell in them after His departure, and they needed to understand what their spiritual relationship to Him meant for the future. They were to bear much spiritual fruit by the power they draw from Him daily, and by their fruit they were to glorify God. Fruit is mentioned three times in John 15:2. The husbandman takes away the unfruitful branch. It is fruitlessness that seals the fate of the branch. It may have leaves. It may be beautiful and good for shade, but it is not fulfilling its purpose of fruitfulness. Fruitful and unfruitful are absolute alternatives—either/or. There is a taking away in either case, either the branch itself or that which hinders its increase in fruitfulness.

C. Cleansing Through the Word (John 15:3-4)

That cleansing which first made the disciples Christ's followers should be distinguished from the constant abiding in Christ. Jesus said, *"You are already clean because of the word which I have spoken to you."* Christ called the disciples to be followers of Him, and they responded to His call. They chose to identify with Jesus and to leave all and follow Him. This is justification: the Word received and embraced by faith. There is a cleansing which follows. *"Abide in Me, and I in you. As the branch cannot bear fruit of itself, unless it abides in the vine, neither can you, unless you abide in Me."* *"In me"* denotes our faith in Christ for salvation and our union with Him in justification. *"I in you"* expresses a closer union, in the hour of full surrender, to abide in us by the Holy Spirit as our Lord and life. This is the secret of sanctification, communion, power and fruitfulness. After this union and communion is formed, it must be maintained by watchfulness and obedient dependence and fellowship. Pruning is part of the divine discipline. This is the Father's thoughtful, patient care as the heavenly Husbandman. There must be obedience on our part if we would abide in Christ. Verse 10 says, *"If you keep My commandments, you will abide in My love."* Verse 14 says, *"You are My friends if you do whatever I command you."*

D. The Meaning of Abiding in Christ (John 15:4)

Abiding in Christ means to believe in Him and constantly receive from Him grace for grace, day by day, in ever greater fullness. The branch remains and receives life from the vine, and this is the way it develops and grows. This is mediated by His Word, to know and be obedient to His Word. It brings us to the importance of knowing what His Word has to say to us through diligent study. People do not respond or act on what they do not know. It is a deterrent to the influences that would draw us away

from Jesus and substitute something in place of Him and His Word; it will constantly respond with good works or fruit. With the true knowledge of His Word and faith in Jesus Christ, we should pray without ceasing that through the Holy Spirit and His grace, by means of studying and practicing God's Word, He will strengthen us from day to day and keep us faithful to the end. We have His promise that He will be with us and remain in us. We in Him and He in us always go together. Jesus Himself is in us when we, by faith, abide in Him. A branch bears no fruit except it abide in the vine, and there is a note of warning, *"neither can you, unless you abide in Me."* The cause is that there is a willful turning away from the blessing and privilege of abiding in Christ and bearing fruit. To make ourselves something else besides the branch abiding in the vine is a serious matter.

E. The Importance of Abiding in Christ (John 15:5)

Jesus Christ is the vine and the disciples are the branches, and to be severed from the vine results in helplessness. *"You can do nothing."* Abiding in Christ and experiencing His grace always results in *"much fruit."* The alternative is separation from Jesus; there is no fruit.

F. The Consequences of Choosing not to Abide in Christ (John 15:6)

"If anyone does not abide in Me, he is cast out as a branch and is withered; and they gather them and throw them into the fire, and they are burned." This is a text that many people would like to extract because of the reality of it. It creates an inner soul wrestling. The unforgettable example is Judas. It places responsibility on each individual. This further explains John 15:2 by stating the reality. The condition of expectancy intimates that some will choose not to remain in Jesus. Jesus never refuses to remain in us if we remain in Him. It is never a question of His willingness but of ours. He casts no one out, but some cast Him off.

The darkest part of the apostasy is the fate of the unfruitful branches with the warning that it implies for us. We note five stages: he is thrown out; is withered; they gather them; they throw them into the fire; they are burned. The unfruitful branch that is taken away by the *"vinedresser"* is cast forth like the branch cut off from a natural vine. The inner separation is followed by the outer separation. The one who has chosen not to abide in Christ is one who no longer reads or obeys the Word of God. He no longer enjoys spiritual fellowship and worship. He chooses to separate Himself from the fellowship of other believers. The text only explains the results, not the steps, by which they are reached. This one is different from the hypocrite who may be in the church but never has been a branch in the vine, never has been a part of the fellowship in a true sense.

"And is withered." Life disappears. This may be a process of time, gradually shriveling and drying up. How terrible to be aware of one in this condition. Not that we are to be judges, but God's Word identifies such a one. The final gathering is made by the angels at the time of judgment. The wood of the branches is fit for only two things: to bear fruit or to burn.

II. The Fruits of Abiding In Christ
(John 15:7-12)
A. Holiness, Usefulness, Prayer, Joy and Love

First of all, we need to recognize that these are fruits and not works of the flesh and the will. They come from the life within, just as the vine bears fruit without effort and the fruit grows for gladness. The first of these fruits is holiness (verse 3). *"You are already clean because of the word which I have spoken to you."* All true holiness must come from the indwelling life of Christ. The next fruit is usefulness. This is expressed by the figure of *"much fruit."* Fruit is reproductive, some thirty, some sixty and some one-hundred fold. *"By this My Father is glorified, that you bear much fruit."* Another fruit is answered prayer (verse 7). *"If you abide in Me, and My words abide in you, you will ask what you desire, and it shall be done for you."* No limit exists for the vine. The only limit is in our faith, which may not ask even though it has the right to ask. Another fruit of abiding in Christ is the fullness of joy (verse 11). It is not only that we should know the love of Jesus and have that love, but also that we have joy in Him. Fruit for the Master brings joy to our lives. If His life is in us we will experience His joy. Love is also a fruit of the Christ-life. Jesus said, *"that you love one another as I have loved you."* This is love that is demonstrated in action.

B. Discipleship Which Glorifies God
(John 15:8)

"Much fruit" on our part and established discipleship glorify God, who sent Jesus to be our Saviour and Lord. The Father is gloried in the fact that the disciples bear much fruit. God is glorified in the work of His Son, and He is also glorified in the work of believers who abide in the Son. Discipleship is a growing and developing way of life.

After expressing the obligations of discipleship, Jesus then concentrated on His love for them. His love for them is like the Father's love for Him. Jesus admonished them to continue in His love. This love Jesus had for the disciples was evidenced in all His relationships to them and in dealing with them. Jesus wanted this love to ever shine upon His disciples, that they would be instruments to carry out its saving purposes in the world.

C. True Discipleship and Obedience
(John 15:10)

In verse 10, Jesus returns to the thought of keeping the commandments. It is interesting to see how the obligations resting on the disciples intertwine with the thought of blessings that there are in Christ. This requires simple obedience. It is when we keep His commandments that we abide in His love. Christ kept the Father's commandments, and He abides continually in the Father's love. Jesus has spoken these things to His disciples that His joy might be in them. He looks for their joy to be complete, to be filled. The joy of which He speaks comes from whole-hearted obedience. Jesus said, *"love one another."* It is only when we abide in Christ, in His Word, in His love, that we shall be able to keep on loving one another. The disciples are not merely to be attached to each other, devoted to each other, helpful to each other. Many who are not disciples show this kind of love, even calling each other brothers. To love as Jesus loved is to see what He sees, the soul's needs, the eternal interests. We must also have the same will and purpose toward others that Jesus showed toward us, the kind of love that was willing to give all that the work of God might be accomplished in salvation through His grace and mercy and through God's spiritual gifts in the ministry of His work. So many of us live selfishly today. The most important things in life to us center around "I," "my" and "me." What would our churches, world and homes be like if we knew the true meaning of Christ's love for us and His love for the world? Jesus said that this love and obedience was an identity as to true discipleship.

D. The Supreme Evidence of Love (John 15:13-15)

Jesus' giving His life was supreme evidence of love. He laid down His life for the sake of His friends. Christians today are reaping all the benefits of this love, and in turn are to let this same love fill their hearts and be willing to prove their love by making the same kind of sacrifice for each other. Jesus says our love for our brethren must be willing to rise to this height, thus following His example.

Jesus said to the disciples, *"You are My friends if you do whatever I command you."* "Friends" means to love with affection and denotes an affectionate relationship. The condition on which the relationship exists and continues is that the disciples keep doing the Lord's bidding. How long Jesus had been calling His disciples *"friends"* is not indicated. The slave or bondservant simply receives his master's orders and carries them out. His master would not confide in him all his plans and purposes. With the disciples it was different. They were friends of Jesus in the fullest sense of the word, for Jesus confided to them all that He heard from the Father: that He was to be the Light and the Life of the world; He was to make the blind to see and to satisfy the thirsty, to make the dead alive, and now He is giving His very life for the world and then returning to the Father. He is coming again to abide with them through the Holy Spirit and is returning at the last day to judge the world and to take His own to Himself into the heavenly mansions.

Daily Bible Study Questions for Group Discussion

Note: Read notes and scripture references before answering the questions. Some questions are for those more advanced in Bible study. Try to answer all questions but don't be discouraged if some seem a little hard. Unless otherwise instructed, use Bible only in answering questions.

FIRST DAY: Read notes on Lesson #23.

1. What are the privileges Jesus said would be given to those who abide in Him?

2. What are the essential conditions for the enjoyment of these privileges?

3. What was the most interesting part of the notes?

SECOND DAY: Read John 15:17-27.

4. List as many reasons you can find why His disciples might be expected to meet hatred in the world?

5. Thinking of our past lessons in John, what reason would Jesus have for stating that the world hated Him, stating this as a fact, not as an assumption? Give references.

6. In this passage, what do you think He means by **"the world"**? With what is it in contrast?

THIRD DAY: Read Acts 6:8-15; Acts 7.

7. In using the above references, how would you characterize the history of the nation that was so violently opposed to Jesus?

8. How does the incident recorded in **Acts 7** enact the very treatment that Jesus said would be the consequences of the disciples' identity with Him?

9. Make a list of some of the advantages of the nation of Israel that should have given them a great love for God because of His past mercies to them.

10. What was the underlying cause of the Jews' hatred toward Jesus and His servants?

FOURTH DAY: Read John 15:22-24.

11. What two forms of Christ's manifestation of His divine nature did He put before the world?

12. What serious consequences resulted from the Jews' rejection of the manifestations of Christ? Give verses.

13. How do the words and works of Christ affect us today as far as human responsibility goes?

FIFTH DAY: Read John 15:25-27.

14. What fact is stated which shows that the rejection of Jesus and the hatred for Him lacked any reasonable foundation?

15. In what way does Jesus remind His disciples that He would give to them the comfort and help they need in a hostile world?

16. What can we learn from our text as to the persons of the Godhead?

17. In what way were the disciples to have a particular function in bearing witness for Jesus Christ?

SIXTH DAY: Read John 16:1-4.

18. From **John 15**, what in particular had Jesus told His disciples that would prepare them for their future work in the world?

19. (a) What expression shows the intensity of that hatred for the disciples as well as for all Christians?

    (b) To what does Jesus attribute this conduct?

20. Why was it not necessary for Jesus to give this information to the disciples sooner?

Notes

The Disciples and the World
John 15:16-27 - John 16:1-4

I. Bearing Fruit in a Hostile World
(John 15:16)
A. Christian Discipleship

In the first verse of John 15, we studied about true union with Christ resulting in a fruitful life. In the last verses in this same chapter, Jesus tells somewhat of the cost involved with individual commitment to the work of Christ and our identity with Him. It must have been very special for the disciples that Christ said to them, *"You did not choose Me, but I chose you and appointed you that you should go and bear fruit."* I believe this is what Christ would say to all Christians, for in His great plan of redemption, He made provision for all men everywhere in choosing the cross. He chose this for the little band of disciples, the inner circle, and what He chose for them He chose for all. God, in His sovereignty, knew many would reject His provision of salvation through His Son Jesus Christ. God has also purposed that every believer be conformed to the image of His Son. There is a work in God's plan for each of His children, that of being fruitful for the kingdom. He has ordained this and set us apart for that special ministry. Have you asked Him where that place is and how best you can effect that ministry?

B. Christ Calls and Prepares Us for His Work

Christ ordains us and also qualifies us for this work, and we are given this promise: *"And that your fruit should remain."* The ministry we do prayerfully for the Lord is lasting. How many good works that we do through self-effort are only temporary. God's glory must always be our goal. *"By this My Father is glorified, that you bear much fruit."* The disciples probably didn't fully realize at this time the special position God had for them, but in the future days, following the resurrection and ascension and the Day of Pentecost, they would understand. Fruit is the spontaneous, natural manifestation of the life within. The one who has the life and love of Christ cannot help producing fruit. It is the unrestrained out-pouring of a heart at peace with God, filled with the love of Christ, and stimulated by the presence and power of the Holy Spirit. What is true of the fruit of the disciples is also true of the fruit of the Christian today. Every fruit of the spirit contains two parts, that of holiness and that of usefulness. Let us not only enjoy the spiritual blessings that we personally enjoy, but let us communicate them to others.

C. "Love," the Motivating Factor
(John 15:17)

This is the same thought presented in verse 12. *"This is My commandment, that you love one another."* The work is all love: love in its hidden source, the love of the Father and in its manifestation, the love of Christ, and lastly, in its full outpouring, the love of believers for each other. Love is its root, its stem, its fruit. It forms the essential characteristics of the new kingdom, whose power and conquests will be the results of the contagion of love. This is why Christ left no other law but that of love to those who had by faith become members of the body of Christ.

II. The Disciples Face the World
(John 15:18-25)
A. Unregenerate Humanity
(John 15:18-25)

Friendship with Jesus means enmity with the world. To hate evil is right, but evil was not the object of their hate. It was the good that was embodied in Jesus Christ. This enmity was obvious from Bethlehem to Calvary, and this hatred for the Son of God developed into persecution. The history of true Christians in all ages has been one of persecution. It was a hatred without cause. The eternal principles of Christianity expose their deep-rooted prejudices and exposed their wickedness. In John 15:19, Christ told the disciples the reason for their hatred, *"If you were of the world, the world would love its own. Yet because you are not of the world, but I chose you out of the world, therefore the world hates you."* Christ forewarned His disciples by urging them to love one another. A strong mutual love among believers would be vital, as the enemy was strong in their hostility against them.

B. Jesus Warns the Disciples to Expect Persecution (John 15:20)

"Remember the word that I said to you." The disciples were to remember this word of Jesus. He had made these His very own. It is better and higher to be slaves of this glorious Master, who makes His slaves His confidants and friends, than to remain imaginary masters of ourselves but in reality slaves of the devil. Belonging as we do to Jesus as our Master, it is certain that we cannot hope to enjoy a better fate than He had with regard to the world. *"A servant is not greater than his master. If they persecuted Me, they will also persecute you."* Did they persecute Jesus? Did they keep His word? So will they do with the disciples and their word. Here we see how the hatred of the world actually shows itself by persecution, back of which lies hostile unbelief.

C. The Inner Cause of the World's Hostility (John 15:21)

From the manifestations of the world's hatred, Jesus turns to its inner cause. The world would have hatred for the disciples of Christ because of His name. All that happens to the disciples is because of Jesus. It is by "His name" that He comes to men — He and all He is and has for men. Thus we believe in "His name," confess "His name," pray in "His name," and Jesus told the disciples they would suffer because of "His name." As Christians we have taken His name, and it is this that the world opposes. All that the name represents in Jesus Christ as Saviour and Master of our life, they will oppose. The more the world sees of Christ in us, the more it turns against us. The Christian represents that which is in opposition to the world. It is sad to see people who profess to be Christians compromising with the world to solicit its friendship. With discipleship as Jesus taught it, there is no room for compromise. Compromise never wins a person to Jesus Christ.

Yet Jesus said that back of all this aversion is still something deeper. The world will persecute the Christian *"because they know not Him who sent Me."* This does not excuse the world. The world does not know the true God who sent His Son to redeem the world. The world has its own god and fights against the true and living God and His Son Jesus Christ, and persecutes those who confess Him. This is the inner reason for the world's hatred.

D. "They Have no Excuse for their Sin" (John 15:22-25)

"If I had not come and spoken to them, they would have no sin." Now they have no excuse for their sin. Christ, "Messiah," came and revealed Himself to the world but they would not hear Him. This robbed them of all excuses, and they stand guilty before God. No unbeliever is able to find even the shadow of an excuse for rejecting Him. This blindness which had prevailed throughout the entire history of the Jewish nation might still have been forgiven them if at this time they had received Jesus. But their rejection showed a hatred for God as well as for His Son. The former sin of Israel, its long resistance to God, would have been forgiven had they not rejected their Messiah and Saviour. In this rejection there is hatred, and in this hatred toward Him, the Jewish malignity reveals itself as hatred of God. No man is able to hate only Jesus; no man is able to separate Jesus and the Father. It is foolish for a man to think He can love, honor and obey God and yet reject Jesus Christ.

The words of Jesus alone should have been sufficient to produce faith, but then Jesus added His works to His Words. *"If I had not done among them the works which no one else did, they would have no sin."* Jesus used the works He had done as convincing proof against unbelief. The Jewish leaders dreaded the effect of these miracles, and for this reason wanted Jesus out of the way. *"But now they have seen and also hated both Me and My Father."* God sent Jesus to do these mighty works. Jesus said in verse 25 that they hated Him without cause. Jesus applied to Himself what David uttered concerning himself in Psalm 35:9. The words that fit David in his suffering fit Jesus even more perfectly. In pointing to the Jewish law, Jesus indicated that the Jews who had this as their law should have been warned against this causeless hatred. They read their own law with blind eyes. Those who hate without a cause carry their verdict in their sin.

III. The Believers' Power to Be Overcomers in a Hostile World
(John 15:26-27)

A. The Power of the Holy Spirit

Jesus told the disciples how they would be hated by the world just as it hated Him, and that hate was without cause. He also implied that the disciples should face the world and its hostilities rather than withdraw from it. Jesus gave the disciples the promise that the Holy Spirit would be with them, that they may boldly testify of Him. The hatred of the world would go on because they would continue to give testimony of Jesus. Nothing is said about the success of this testimony or how it would win many from the world to faith in Jesus Christ; it will not be in vain but will bear *"much fruit."* Success is God's part; faithfulness is ours. We have a tendency to mark success with bigness in numbers and finances, but not so with God. Being faithful to the ministry to which God has called us is the most important thing. God gives the fruit. One faithful servant plants, one waters, but God gives the increase. This fruit, Jesus said, would remain. It is interesting to note here that after saying that the Father would give the Holy Spirit at Jesus' request, He now says He will send the Holy Spirit. The Father's giving is accomplished by the Son's sending: the Son's sending is accomplished by the Father's giving. The Holy Spirit is called the Spirit of Truth because of His work in the world, testifying to the world concerning Jesus. So the work will be accomplished by One as great as Jesus Himself, One Who is at the side of the disciples, working ceaselessly just as Jesus had worked at the side of the disciples until this time.

The disciples also needed to testify of all they had seen and heard while they were with Jesus. The testimony of the Holy Spirit and of the disciples goes into the world as one. He and they are joined together to give the message of the gospel of Christ. The disciples possessed a treasure which was peculiar to them: the historical knowledge of the ministry of Jesus from its beginning to its end. The Holy Spirit teaches us the meaning of these facts. But without the Holy Spirit, this historical testimony of the apostles would simply amount to knowledge which would not affect the lives of men as a quickening power of spiritual life and service. Without the historical facts, the Holy Spirit's work would be unfruitful. Both are necessary for salvation through Christ and the power of the Holy Spirit to give us power for ministry and to teach us all truth as Jesus said.

B. The Disciples Face the World
(John 16:1-4)

"These things I have spoken to you, that you should not be made to stumble." that they should not be caught unaware. Jesus did not want His disciples to suddenly discover that discipleship means the vicious hatred of the world. Jesus fully informed them of what it really means to be a disciple; He told them all of its hard and painful potential.

Jesus told them of two of the worst forms of persecution the world is capable of doing. To be excommunicated from the synagogue, in a land where all were Jews, amounted to being a religious outcast. Because fanatic hatred had far-reaching implications in the community of religious fanatics, the extremity of their fanaticism would be murder of such a one, thinking they were doing God a favor by killing the disciples of Jesus Christ. It seems incredible that people who have the Scriptures can so reverse what the Scriptures teach.

The explanation Jesus gave for this is in John 16:3, *"And these things they will do to you because they have not known the Father nor Me."* This is not said to excuse, but to reveal their guilt. Jesus was the final revelation God gave to the Jews, and they rejected the knowledge of the Old Testament Scriptures and therefore rejected the promised Messiah in Jesus Christ. Jesus Christ revealed the Father in all His redemptive and saving love to a world that knew not God nor His Son. The nation Israel had made its own god from their own minds and the pagan world around them. Is this not true of the world of unbelief today? What Jesus said to the disciples would prepare them for the hostility of the world. The radical zeal of Paul at the stoning of Stephen, recorded in Acts 7, is an example of the fanaticism as Jesus described it, although in Paul's example we find his ignorance surpassed his hatred. In his heart, hatred of Jesus was not hatred of God.

Jesus spoke of His purpose of making known to the disciples the world's hostility so that when the time came they would remember all that Jesus had told them. It is precious to know that Jesus fortifies us when we need it and gives us the armor just before the battle. *"Because I was with you."* means He was with them visibly and that the hatred was directed toward Him. It was Jesus they wanted to kill, andthe disciples were not considered important. After Jesus would leave them, they would stand alone without the visible presence of Jesus. They will be His representatives, and then they would feel the hatred that Jesus had felt.

Daily Bible Study Questions for Group Discussion

Note: Read notes and scripture references before answering the questions. Some questions are for those more advanced in Bible study. Try to answer all questions but don't be discouraged if some seem a little hard. Unless otherwise instructed, use Bible only in answering questions.

FIRST DAY: Read notes on Lesson #24.

1. What reasons are given in **John 15** for the Christian being hated by the world?

2. What two sources of comfort does a Christian have that will equip him for the work God has for him to do?

3. Can Christians create some self-inflicted problems in the world through lack of wisdom. If so give examples.

4. What reason did Jesus give for not earlier disclosing to the disciples the painful aspect of discipleship?

SECOND DAY: Read John 16:5-15.

5. In reading **John 14:28, John 16:5 and John 16:10**, to what is Jesus giving emphasis?

6. Jesus had been three years with His disciples, and now He is leaving them. For what two things in particular did Jesus seem to give a gentle reproof to them?

7. In referring to **John 16:7-15**, to what two groups of people will the Holy Spirit direct His work?

THIRD DAY:

8. With what three subjects does the conviction of the Holy Spirit deal?

9. In analyzing the three subjects resulting from the conviction of the Holy Spirit, how could you identify each with unbelief?

10. What indication is there in these verses of Jesus' love and concern for the feeling of His disciples?

11. From **verses 8 to 15 of John, chapter 16**, what are the three operations of the Holy Spirit concerning:
     (a) the world

     (b) the disciples

     (c) Jesus

12. List the advantages to the disciples resulting from Jesus' return to the Father.

FOURTH AND FIFTH DAYS: Read John 16:16-24.

13. What do you think puzzled the disciples about Jesus saying that:
     (a) *"A little while, and you will not see Me"*

(b)   *"and again a little while, and you will see Me; and, 'because I go to the Father'."*

14. What illustration did Jesus use to teach the disciples that the sorrow they would endure for the sake of the gospel would be fruitful?

15. When you think of the promise Jesus gave to the disciples in **verse 22**, what did He tell them would cause them sorrow and what would be the cause for joy?

16. What would be the disciples' approach to God after Jesus' ascension?

SIXTH DAY: Read John 16:25-33.

17. What put the disciples in a favorable position before the Father?

18. The disciples said, *"By this we believe"* and Jesus said to them, *"Do you now believe?"* What would be the trial and test of this affirmation of discipleship?

19. What words of encouragement did Jesus leave with the disciples?

20. What part of this lesson challenged you spiritually this week?

Notes

EXPLORER'S BIBLE STUDY

The Work of the Holy Spirit
In the World and in the Disciples
John 16:5-33

Introduction

There is a change in the character of the discourses between chapters 14, 15 and 16. The subject of chapter 14 is comfort; chapter 15, that of admonition; chapter 16, that of prediction, indicating what is going to happen. After telling the disciples of the treatment they are to expect from a hostile world, Jesus also tells them of the resources available to them to be overcomers, not only overcomers but a resource that will bring joy to them in place of sorrow.

I.   The Work of the Holy Spirit
(John 16:5-15)

A. To Bring Comfort to the Disciples
(John 16:5-6)

Jesus previously indicated to both Peter and Thomas that He was not leaving for some other place on earth, but was going to the Father (John 14:28). He told them that from the Father He would send another Comforter, the Spirit of Truth. The disciples questioned Jesus as to what he meant by returning to His Father but Jesus did not consider this a justifible inquiry and gave them a gentle reproof. Jesus wanted the disciples to understand the significance of His return for them as He leaves them behind. Peter's previous question was only a selfish exclamation which did not want Jesus to go away alone. The assertion of Thomas was tainted with discouragement because Jesus was leaving them, and they really did not know for sure the *"way"* that Jesus talked about. Jesus is leaving, and for what this will mean to the disciples you would expect they would search for further information. All they could think about at this time was their impending loss, and sorrow had filled their hearts. In the question Jesus asks them, *"But now I go away to Him who sent Me, and none of you asks Me, 'Where are You going?'"* The situation seems to disappoint Jesus. The disciples were concentrating on His departure and what this would mean to them.

It seems they did not comprehend what this would mean both for them and for Jesus. Instead of being comforted with what Jesus had told them, it had the opposite effect.

B. Promise of the Holy Spirit
(John 16:7)

In trying to counteract the sorrow Jesus knew His disciples were feeling, He reassured them of what He had already promised them. *"Nevertheless I tell you the truth. It is to your advantage that I go away; for if I do not go away, the Helper will not come to you; but if I depart, I will send Him to you."* Jesus wanted to remove their sorrow to make room for what He wanted to put in its place. If Jesus should stay with the disciples in visible form as they wanted Him to, then the Holy Spirit would not come, and all that Christ's coming meant, for the greater work for which He had trained His disciples, could not follow. But Jesus said, *"if I depart"* I will send the Holy Spirit to you. With the coming of the Holy Spirit, the great work of salvation would be carried to its consummation to the everlasting joy and glory for the world as well as for the disciples. Jesus must complete His redemptive work by His death, resurrection and ascension so that the Holy Spirit may take this work and by means of the gospel, spread its saving power to the ends of the earth.

C. The Two-fold Work of the Holy
Spirit (John 16:8)

The two-fold work of the Holy Spirit would be toward the world (verses 8-11) and toward the disciples (verses 12-15). Jesus would send the Holy Spirit to the disciples, and He would abide permanently in them. They would be the instruments through whom the Holy Spirit will work. Peter's sermon on the Day of Pentecost is the best commentary of the work of the Holy Spirit. Three thousand were won to Christ through his preaching. All who do not come to Christ and repent of sin stand convicted and guilty before Christ. Conviction deals with three subjects: sin, righteousness and judgment.

1. Concerning Sin
(John 16:9)

Sin, righteousness and judgment all exist. The world certainly knows about sin; the daily news is an indicator of that fact. The world needs something that will convict them of sin. The Holy Spirit supplies this need. The conviction of the Holy Spirit is in regard to one thing and that is in the rejection of Jesus Christ. Not to believe in Jesus is to remain in sin; it means to be lost. To believe in Jesus is to be saved from sin. Therefore the work of the Holy Spirit is to convict the world of its unbelief in Jesus Christ. Only one who really believes will have eternal life. Many people say they believe but have only a vague idea of who Jesus is and who God really is. Conviction reacts in two different ways: it will either bring one to repentance and belief or it will harden the heart of one convicted of sin. Jesus said to the Jews in John 8:24, *"Therefore I said to you that you will die in your sins."* It is possible to over-emphasize the word "sin" and that which concerns sin and fail to see the full significance of the word "believe." The world knows about sin, and it is only by the convicting power of the Holy Spirit that they will turn from their sin. What they need to know is the positive message of Jesus Christ, of what it really means to believe on Him and to be saved from sin. All men are saved through the grace of God, the redemptive work of Jesus Christ His Son, and the convicting power of the Holy Spirit.

2. Concerning Righteousness
(John 16:10)

The world seeks to cover up sin. They love darkness because their deeds are evil, yet they always seek "righteousness" in some form or another. They either make themselves judge of their own case, or when they think of God as the judge, they think of Him as One who deals gently with sin. They have their own schemes for appearing righteous. They think that their good deeds will outweigh their evil. They accept religion that teaches good works as a means of righteousness, and they think this is the way to heaven. The world tries to secure righteousness for itself by efforts of its own. The work of the Holy Spirit is to convict the world in regard to righteousness.

The Jewish world also had a distorted view of righteousness. In pride, Israel had taken its position in opposition to Jesus and rejected Him as One worthy only to die. They ascribed sin to Jesus and righteousness to themselves. Pentecost reversed that sentence; it assigned righteousness to the condemned One of Calvary and sin to the ones who judged Him. Righteousness is the state of the sinner whom God acquits; God alone is the judge. Righteousness has to do with Jesus, His return to the Father, the completion of His work of redemption. The Holy Spirit convicts the sinner that true righteousness is available for him, and only in Him who has passed from the cross and is now in heaven with His Father. *"Nor is there salvation in any other, for there is no other name under heaven given among men by which we must be saved."* (Acts 4:12) Here again, through the conviction of the Holy Spirit, some accept the righteousness; they believe, are justified and are saved. Others just turn aside and remain in their unbelief, continuing with their distorted view of what it means to be truly righteous.

3. Concerning Judgment
(John 16:11)

The world is not yet judged, but it will be convicted in regard to judgment. The Holy Spirit will point the world to its own ruler whose fate is already sealed. He has been judged and that judgment stands fixed. Jesus speaks of the devil's judgment as having been effected, because His own death and resurrection, which brought about the final judgment on the devil, are already at hand and are as certain as if already completed. Satan is moving toward his defeat. In the devil's judgment, the world may see something concerning judgment for itself. The children of the world have submitted to him and he is their ruler. The Holy Spirit is busy gathering in the great harvest of the world of those who have refused to be included in Satan's domain.

D. The Holy Spirit and the Disciples
(John 16:12-15)

Jesus had instructed the disciples on the essential points, but at this time He said He would not elaborate on them out of concern for the disciples. The circumstances would limit their ability to perceive until they received the Holy Spirit, (who Jesus said is the *"Spirit of Truth"*) was given. *"When He, the Spirit of truth, has come, He will guide you into all truth."* Jesus Christ Himself is truth, and Jesus had imparted this to them by His words and works. Now the disciples are given the promise of the Holy Spirit to guide them in this truth. This is a description of the office of the Holy Spirit. Much lay within the circle of the truth Jesus taught; the Holy Spirit would be their teacher and guide. As the Spirit of Truth, this guide is absolutely perfect, like Jesus Himself who is the Truth. When the Holy Spirit came to dwell in the disciples, they were able to bear all He communicated to them.

"He will not speak on His own authority, but whatever He hears He will speak; and He will tell you things to come." This had to do with the source and the substance of the truth which the Spirit communicated to them and to us. The Divine Persons communicate with each other; nothing known to the One is ever hidden from the Other as they are One in essence. The synoptic gospels record what Jesus taught about the future, *"things to come,"* and the Holy Spirit amplified and deepened these things.

The purpose of the Holy Spirit is given in the words, *"And He will glorify Me."* The emphasis is on *"Me."* The work of the Holy Spirit is to glorify Jesus and to place Him before the eyes and hearts of people, to make His Person and work shine before them. *"For He will take of what is Mine and declare it to you."* This refers back to verse 13, *"He will guide you into all truth,"* meaning all the saving realities in Jesus Christ. This is the work of the Holy Spirit, and the entire New Testament is evidence of this work. All things of Jesus are also of the Father; they are identical; they belong to the Father and the Son. It is one substance of truth: the Father has it, the Son sends it, and the Spirit takes it. All three combine in making this blessed treasure our own.

II. Concluding Conversation of Jesus with the Disciples (John 16:16-33)
A. The Little While of Sorrow (John 16:16-24)

In the coming and work of the Holy Spirit, experiencing joy instead of sorrow, the disciples would experience greater advantage in Jesus' return to His Father than if He had stayed and continued His earthly ministry with them. He comforts them with the words that His separation from them would be for *"a little*

while." The first *"little while"* would only be a few hours. Jesus would be taken away from them, put to death and buried. These would be the darkest hours for the disciples, but it would only be for *"a little while."* Until the morning of the resurrection, the disciples would need to cling to the hope of the words of Jesus of His returning to them after a short time. There is difference of opinion as to the meaning of the second *"little while"* because Jesus said, *"and you will see Me; and, because I go to the Father"* Some believe this means from the resurrection until the day of the ascension. Others interpret it to mean the coming of the Holy Spirit at Pentecost, and still others believe it means Jesus is talking about His second advent in the last days. It is not necessary to try to exhaust this in deep theological searching, for no doubt Jesus had in mind the comfort He could give to His disciples in a blessed hope of His presence with them, visible after the resurrection through the Holy Spirit following Pentecost, and then on that last great and wonderful day when all will behold our blessed Redeemer and Lord as He comes again to take us to be with Him throughout eternity.

B. The Disciples' Perplexity (John 16:17-18)

The perplexity among the disciples was caused when Jesus said they would see Him in a little while, and yet He also said He was going to His Father. This going away would remove Him from them. The puzzle was putting together all He said He would do when He went to His Father, and now the statement that it would not be for very long. They were unable to solve the puzzle and said, *"We do not know what He is saying."*

C. Jesus Answers the Disciples' Perplexity (John 16:19-22)

In His wisdom, Jesus replies to the need rather than to the question. He had no difficulty in knowing their perplexity. The puzzle would be solved and the meaning become clear to the disciples in a far better way than words could instruct them at this time.

What Jesus had to say to his disciples was important. He told them that the *"little while"* would be a difficult time for them; they would *"weep and lament"* while the enemies of Christ rejoiced. But Jesus did not end on a note of sorrow. The disciples' sorrow would turn to joy. Jesus gave an illustration that shows them that the same thing can produce entirely different opposites. The birth of a child produces pain and then abounds in joy. The joy is so great that the brief time of anguish is soon forgotten — sorrow made joy. Verse 22 is the simple interpretation of the illustration: *"Therefore you now have sorrow"* but in a little while *"your heart will rejoice, and your joy no one will take from you."* The resurrection brought this promised joy to the disciples and to the world. Little wonder that for the joy of a risen Christ, the disciples could endure all they were subjected to in the world. Jesus Christ and His resurrection is the hope of the world. For the one who experiences this joy, no sacrifice is too costly.

D. Relationship and Privileges of the Disciples (John 16:23-28)

"In that Day" means following the resurrection and the ascension. The disciples had asked Jesus many questions while He was with them. After He was gone from them and His bodily presence no longer was with them, Jesus wanted them to know that they would still have access to Him through the Father. The disciples had no need to pray to Jesus while He was with them because they could commune with Him daily, but after He was gone to His Father, they would pray to the Father in Jesus' name. For Christians, prayer is normally addressed to the Father in the name of Jesus and that prayer is all-prevailing. Because of all Jesus is and does, men receive gifts from the Father. For those who ask the Father in Jesus' name, the promise is that they will receive.

E. In Anticipation of the Day of Victory (John 16:25-33)

As a result of Jesus' teaching, the disciples began to respond positively as they understood better what Jesus was telling them. They declared, *"Now we are sure . . . By this we believe that You came forth from God."* They confessed their faith in their Master. This must have been a real joy and comfort to the heart of Jesus. The disciples had drawn the right conclusions regarding Jesus. This is the last confession of faith the disciples made before the death of Jesus, and in it they confessed the deity of Jesus,

and with this, the saving mission. Jesus fully acknowledges the faith of the disciples in that they believed Jesus came from the Father with all this involved. The disciples very shortly would be scattered and leave Him alone, Him whom they had just confessed. Where would their love, faith, courage and gratitude be? Jesus would be left alone in the hands of His enemies. They would do it and Jesus would bear it. As far as the disciples were concerned, Jesus would be alone, but not so concerning His Father. He would remain with Him.

Jesus revealed why He told the disciples these things. Jesus would leave them, but He promised to them a peace in spite of all they would face in the next hours. It is a gift He gives to His disciples, leaving it as His blessed legacy when He departs from them. Jesus gives peace of which the world does not know. After Jesus promised peace, He told them not to be troubled and afraid. At times the feeling of fear and trouble keeps us from experiencing that peace because we have allowed it to overwhelm us, but nevertheless the peace Christ gives is there, and we will come to recognize it. Jesus wanted His disciples to fight the feeling of depression, to be courageous. No matter what the world does to them, they have peace with God through Jesus Christ. With this, they can face the world's hatred with a cheerful and strong heart. The disciples did not experience this fully until after the Day of Pentecost. Acts 5:41, *"Rejoicing that they were counted worthy to suffer shame for His name."* Jesus said, *"I have overcome the world."* The world cannot and will not prevail because victory is in Jesus, in that the ruler of this world has already been judged and is now to be cast out. Jesus' victory is also that of the disciples, for they are in Him and He in them. It is our faith in Jesus Christ that will cause us to have victory in our lives today. This was Jesus' last discourse with His disciples and now all they needed was the power, courage and joy of it in their hearts, which they would experience *"in a little while."*

Daily Bible Study Questions for Group Discussion

Note: Read notes and scripture references before answering the questions. Some questions are for those more advanced in Bible study. Try to answer all questions but don't be discouraged if some seem a little hard. Unless otherwise instructed, use Bible only in answering questions.

FIRST DAY: Read notes on Lesson #25.

1. Jesus understood all that would happen between this time with the disciples and the coming of the Holy Spirit, but to the disciples it was a time of sorrow and fear. As Jesus tried to prepare His disciples for the dark hours ahead, what are some of the points He emphasized in **John 16**?

2. What privileges and blessings does Jesus say the disciples will enjoy when the Holy Spirit comes? **(See verses 22-27.)**

3. What in particular does Jesus say about prayer? What light does His words throw upon the meaning of *"in My name?"*

4. Jesus sums up what He has been telling His disciples in **John 16:33**. In what two opposing   spheres would the disciples live? What would be their experience in each?

5. What would be the basis of their courage and confidence?

SECOND DAY: Read John 17.

6. From **John 17**, what does Jesus say He had accomplished during His earthly ministry?

7. Give the verses that mark the three divisions in this chapter.
   (1) Christ prays for Himself

   (2) Christ prays for the immediate circle of disciples

   (3) Christ prays for the great company who will afterwards believe

8. How many different titles does Jesus use in addressing God throughout this chapter?

THIRD DAY: Read John 17 (continued).

9. What reciprocal acts are given in the first verses of **John 17**?

10. In previous chapters of John, Jesus spoke of giving eternal life. In **John 17**, He states what receiving and having eternal life means. What is receiving and having eternal life?

11. Make a list of the gifts Jesus received from the Father which He gives to the believer.

12. When Jesus prayed for His disciples, He mentioned four identifying qualities regarding His disciples. What are they?

13. Jesus recognizes in His prayer that the world in which He was leaving His disciples would subject the disciples to dangers. What are His concerns?

14. Jesus gives three kinds of *"oneness"* in His prayer. What are they, and list the verses where found.

FIFTH AND SIXTH DAYS: John 17 (continued).

15. (a) In **verses 22-26**, what evidence is there of Christ's deep love for believers?

(b) How should this affect our lives?

16. What is the means through which men and women come to faith in Christ?

17. List as many verses as you can find in this chapter that will substantiate your answer to question #16.

18. What are the evident results of a church that believes, teaches, lives and confesses the truth we have in the Word?

19. What happens when one gets into the fellowship of a church that deviates in doctrine, life and practice from the Word?

20. There is so much for all of us as we consider this high priestly prayer of Jesus. What part of it was particularly meaningful to you?

Notes

The Intercessory Prayer of Christ
John 17

Introduction

Jesus had both acted and spoken in the previous chapters of the Gospel of John. In the seventeenth chapter Jesus prays. This intercessory prayer is more than a devotional meditation. Its purpose is to deepen and intensify all of His last words to His disciples.

There are three divisions to this chapter which are easy to identify. We will consider each.

(1) Jesus' prayer for Himself (John 17:1-5)
(2) Jesus' prayer for His disciples (John 17:6-19)
(3) Jesus' prayer for future believers in the world (John 17:20-26)

I. Jesus' Prayer for Himself
(John 17:1-5)

A. Jesus Prays to the "Father"
(John 17:1,5)

In His petition, Jesus uses the word *"Father,"* an appropriate address for the Son to use in this circumstance. It is also used in verses 21 and 24. In verse 11, Jesus uses *"Holy Father"* and in verse 25, *"Righteous Father." "Father, the hour has come"* means that His hour is now: the hour for which Jesus came into the world, the time for His death, resurrection and ascension. The time has come for the Father to glorify the Son that the Son may glorify the Father. Paul said in his letter to the Philippians (2:9), *"Therefore God also has highly exalted Him and given Him the name which is above every name, that at the name of Jesus every knee should bow, of those in heaven, and of those on earth, and of those under the earth, and that every tongue should confess that Jesus Christ is Lord, to the glory of God the Father."* The Father is to exalt Jesus by investing His human nature with the unlimited use of the divine attributes, to effect the purpose that the Son may make the glorious attributes of the Father radiate

throughout the world through the work of the Holy Spirit in the gospel and in the church. So that God may complete what He began, He will now glorify Jesus. Jesus and the Father are in absolute harmony as to Christ's mission of redeeming the world. This the disciples would hear as Jesus prayed aloud in their presence: that the Father gave to Jesus *"authority over all flesh,"* the entire human race — rule and dominion over all men. This was a gift of the Father which the Son assumed in the incarnation. He has power to give life eternal, the life of eternal salvation, to all whom the Father gives to Him. This grace is intended for all men, and none are excluded by the giving of the Father nor of Jesus. No limitations are made. Only by rejection do unbelievers exclude themselves from the gift of Jesus and from receiving the gift of life.

B. The Definition of Eternal Life
(John 17:3)

"And this is eternal life, that they may know You, the only true God, and Jesus Christ whom You have sent." This verse does not define the nature of eternal life, but describes in what its reception and its possession consist. He has spoken of giving this life; He now states the meaning of receiving and possessing. To know the Father and Jesus Christ, who is the only way to the Father, refers not to mere abstract knowledge, but to joyful acknowledgment of His sovereignty, and acceptance of His love and fellowship with His person through His word to us, and through prayer. When one experiences eternal life, one has fellowship with God in His only begotten Son, Jesus the Saviour.

C. Jesus Completes His Work on Earth (John 17:4-5)

Christ glorified God by His person, by His life of perfect obedience, by His miracles, by His passion, and by His doctrine. Jesus did all of this by completing the work the Father gave Him to do. This work was for the benefit of men; it was for their redemption and for the glorification of God. The crowning point of this work is in His atoning death. Jesus did not consider this a burden, but a loving gift to Him on the part of the Father.

After the earthly part of the work was completed, the heavenly part of His work could begin. Jesus does not request a reward for His work. By being glorified Himself, Jesus glorified the Father among all men of all ages. By being glorified, Jesus brought to eternal life and glory all whom the Father had given Him. Jesus asked to be in the heavenly glory with the Father as He was with Him before the creation. Now it is the Father who will glorify Him with true glory in the cross and that which follows.

II. Jesus' Prayer for His Disciples
(John 17:6-19)

A. Christ's Work upon Earth with the Disciples (John 17:6-8)

This prayer gives us a glimpse of how Jesus regarded His disciples. It is not just a cold intellectual estimate of the disciples, but shows His profound love for them. Now that He is leaving them, He can place them in the care of a loving Father. One great part of the work of Christ on earth lies completed in the eleven disciples. The eleven were the ones Jesus had prepared to be sent out into the world as His apostles, for whom He prays in a special way. These eleven men were given to Jesus by the Father. They were given to Jesus out of the world, for by natural birth they were part of the world. The eleven previously had been believing Israelites. Six of them had been followers of John the Baptist, which resulted in their becoming followers of Jesus. What the Old Covenant had promised they had found in Jesus. Jesus adds the evidence of this by saying, *"And they have kept Your word."* The words Jesus had spoken to them as from the Father they had received, and believed that Jesus was sent to them from the Father.

B. Jesus' Request on Behalf of the Disciples (John 17:9-19)

Jesus makes request for the disciples and not for the world. This special intercession deals with believers because they are recipients of the blessings which the Father has for His children. In this prayer,

Jesus dwells on the relationship of the disciples to Himself. The unbelieving world would have no interest in the blessings He was asking. Luther says, "What must be asked for the world is that it should be converted, not that it should be kept and sanctified." The world is to be reached through His disciples, and for them Jesus makes His petition.

In verse 10 of John 17, we see the oneness of the Father and the Son; two Persons (*"Mine"* and *"Yours"*), a union exceeding our comprehension. *"And all Mine are Yours, and Yours are Mine, and I am glorified in them."* All that is the Father's is equally the possession of the Son Jesus. We may say that all we have belongs to God, but we cannot say all God has belongs to us. God the Father and God the Son have a purpose which results in mutuality, all this belongs equally to both. In this "Oneness" of Father and Son, the disciples belonged to God though they were given to Jesus. Jesus said, *"And I am glorified in them."* It was this that the disciples believed: that Jesus came from God and was commissioned by Him, and they recognized Him for who He was and trusted in Him.

C. Jesus' First Petition for His Disciples (John 17:11)

Jesus was leaving His disciples in the world; He would be leaving them in a matter of hours. We have had a glimpse of how precious the disciples were to Jesus as well as to the Father. We, as disciples of Christ, need to realize that we also are precious to God and to Christ. Jesus ever lives and makes intercession for us before the throne. If we would remember this, it would help us through the times of discouragement we all encounter in the work of Christ. Discouragement is Satan's tool, and we need to look beyond to the throne of God, knowing that Jesus cares and is interceding for us. Jesus said, *"But these are in the world, and I come to You, Holy Father, keep through Your name those whom You have given Me, that they may be one as We are."* (one in light, life and love). The disciples would be exposed to danger when Jesus left them in the world. The Holy Father is in contrast to the unholiness the disciples will be subjected to in the world. God is holy and is absolutely opposed to all sin. By His grace He works to save men from sin, separates them from the world, and keeps them for Himself as separate and holy. Jesus prayed, *"Keep through Your name those whom You* prayed, *"Keep through Your name those whom You have given Me."* In verse 6, Jesus says the disciples had guarded the Word, and now He asks the Father to keep them faithful to their commitment in the word and work of Christ. The purpose of keeping the disciples *"through Your name"* is *"that they may be one, as We are"*: one body, over against the world. All believers are one spiritually by their living relationship to a living God. The same living Word and *"name,"* the same faith and life in Christ, is in all believers. Jesus prayed that this oneness of the disciples would be guarded and kept in the world by the Heavenly Father. This oneness and unity of purpose can be endangered by any teaching or doctrine contrary to the Word. The entire prayer is that we may be kept in oneness by keeping the Word.

D. Jesus' Watchful Care over His Disciples (John 17:13)

While Jesus was with His disciples, He guarded them as a good shepherd guards his sheep. Through His daily teaching and ministry they were close to Him and He could watch over them, but now they would need the watchful care of the Heavenly Father. *"And none of them is lost except the son of perdition, that the Scripture might be fulfilled."* Jesus had ministered to Judas, as he had done with others, to the very end. The *"son of perdition"* bears a stamp of character rather than destiny. Judas was characterized by "lostness," not that he was predestined to be lost. Christ had kept the disciples so that none was lost. Concerning Judas, there is the consideration that the Father's will was done both in the eleven and in the one, for Scripture was fulfilled. The reference to fulfilling Scripture brings out the thought of divine purpose. This does not mean that Judas acted without intention or awareness. He was a responsible person and acted freely. But God used his evil act to bring about His purpose. God's will in the end was done in the betrayal of Christ to be crucified. How much better it would have been if Judas had fled to the cross rather than choose to take his own life. People make choices. God never makes us robots. We choose to obey or disobey. We choose godliness or worldliness. We choose life in Jesus Christ or death by following Satan. These are simple conclusions, but we need to know that God holds individuals responsible for their choices no matter how much we would like to place the blame on others or Satan. There is no

"keeping in God's name" independent of "keeping God's Word."

E. Jesus Prays for God's Plan to Be Fulfilled (John 17:13)

"That they may have My joy fulfilled in themselves." The disciples, who are to remain in the world for the great work they are to do, are to have in their hearts the very joy that fills the heart of Jesus, and the measure of this joy is complete. It is to be like a vessel that has been filled to the brim from which they may draw at any time. Having the true source of joy, and this in full measure, the rejoicing will follow. *"The joy of the Lord is the strength of His people"* (Nehemiah 8:10). The disciples are to have not only courage and peace, but the true source of joy and the happiness it will give them.

F. Jesus Prays that the Disciples Will Be Kept from Evil in the World (John 17:14-16)

Jesus left the disciples with the divine gift of the Word. Now the thought goes beyond what this gift has made of the disciples to what the world has done to them as a result. *"And the world has hated them because they are not of the world."* The spiritual nature of the disciples had been changed by the Word. This made them foreigners to the world. By natural birth they were of the world, but by the new birth through the Word they had forsaken the world. The world recognized that this came as a result of their association with Jesus and they hated Jesus; therefore they would hate His disciples and all those in the future who would become believers. Our problem today is that the Christian has identified so closely with the world that the world does not recognize an identity with Jesus Christ. The hatred of the world was intensified when the disciples preached and taught the Word. The hatred of the world against the disciples is inspired by Satan. The work of the disciples is to war not only against flesh and blood, but against demon spirits with the *"evil one"* as their head (Ephesians 6:13 and 16). Our protection is to be directed against his fiery darts. This is the protection for which Jesus now prays.

G. Jesus Prays for Sanctification for the Disciples (John 17:17-19)

"Sanctify them by Your truth. Your word is truth." Sanctify means "to set apart for God." We

are to separate from the world and be devoted only to Him. With the disciples, the prayer of Jesus would be for the sanctifying of the Father, that they might be kept wholly separate from the world. *"The truth"* is the substance itself with which the sanctifying work proceeds, the sanctifying power of the Word. Those who see *"the truth"* that saves and sanctifies by going to the Word will find that Word is true on every point and in every respect. Truth corresponds with holiness. By means of *"the truth"* alone and of the Word, whose essential quality is *"truth,"* can the *"Holy Father sanctify us."* Jesus at first prayed *"keep them in Your own name,"* and now *"sanctify them by Your truth."* All of God's Word is truth: the Word of the Old Testament and the revelation that Jesus added in person with the promise of its perfect preservation through the Holy Spirit.

Jesus, who Himself was sent into the world by the Father, now sends forth His disciples into the world. Jesus came as He was sent and fulfilled God's plan and purpose through Calvary, and now the disciples are used to complete God's work on earth through the power of the Holy Spirit. So it is today. God's work is carried forth through believers, called and commissioned by God to faithfulness to Jesus Christ and to the Word. It is only as we study the Word that we know what God expects of us and of what our commission really consists. Knowledge places us in the position of responsibility. God gave His Word to us that we might act upon it. We are to show forth the praises of Him who has called us out of the kingdom of darkness into His marvelous light (I Peter 2:9).

"And for their sakes I sanctify Myself, that they also may be sanctified by the truth." Jesus is speaking of a sanctifying in which He is now engaged. Jesus is going to the Father; He prays to be glorified. By His death, He enters into His glorious heavenly mission in which His world-wide work will begin when He sends the Holy Spirit to be with the disciples in a spiritual presence. For this Jesus now sanctifies Himself by voluntarily entering His sacrificial and atoning death. Jesus Himself must set Himself apart. He must give Himself freely. Apart from this, the mission of the disciples would not be possible. The sanctification of the disciples proceeds from what Jesus now does for them.

III. Christ's Prayer for Future Believers in the World
(John 17:20-26)
A. Christ's Prayer for Oneness
(John 17:20-23)

The eleven disciples sent forth into the world would not be sent in vain. Sanctified and filled with the power of the Holy Spirit, they would bring thousands to faith in Jesus Christ regardless of the opposition of the world. In Jesus' prayer, He makes a distinction between the apostles and future believers. *"I do not pray for these alone, but also for those who will believe in Me through their word."* Future believers would become believers through the word of the apostles, through the teaching and writing of the apostles, God's means of communication, producing faith and making believers. They were the special agents for disseminating and transmitting the Word following the ascension of Christ to His Father. In reality, it is God's Word which is *"truth."* The Word is the vital means and roots of faith. Is it any wonder that when the church does not preach and teach the Word of God that the church is weak, empty and ineffective in the world? They stand for nothing, and consequently fall for most any doctrine that suits their own false standard of philosophy. It is dangerous to be ignorant of the Word or to alter or falsify it in any way. The Word given to the church through the apostles is the foundation of the church for all ages. The legacy they left in the inspired writings of the New Testament, preached and taught, still leads many to believe in Jesus Christ and to follow Him. For these Jesus prays, "That they all may be one" — one with the Father and with Jesus Christ and with the Holy Spirit. *"That they be one even as We"*: one body, one spiritual unit, the disciples and all future believers in opposition to the world. This oneness is not a mere oneness, national, racial or political, but will bear the divine stamp: a oneness in the true God, in union with Him. This is a growing experience, of coming to Christ, giving ourselves to Him in believing faith, prayer and the study of His Word. When our understanding of the Word grows, the inner power of our faith in the Word will likewise grow. We grow to be more and more what Jesus wants us to be. The more we have of the Word in our hearts by faith and therefore ruling our lives, the more perfect is our oneness. We are as much one with each other and with God and with Jesus Christ as we believe, teach, live and confess all that is in the Word. Deviation from the Word mars and disrupts our oneness. It is not the prerogative of society to change God's Word at its whim. God has spoken and we are to teach and preach that Word.

Jesus does not intercede for the world, but the world is the object of His love. His death on the cross was the price paid for their redemption, for all men everywhere of all ages. He prayed *"that the world may believe that You sent Me."* ..... *"And have loved them."* This does not mean that the whole world will finally believe, for many will not believe in spite of the Word being brought to them. The responsibility of the church today is, and has been ever since its inception, to bring the Word to men. We need to pray as Jesus prayed for the complete oneness of the church in the Word.

B. The Conclusion of Christ's Prayer (John 17:24-25)

The closing verses of Christ's prayer contain no more petitions. Christ's will for believers is stated in verse 24. *"Father, I desire that they also whom You gave Me may be with Me where I am."* Death would soon take Jesus from the disciples, but this would only be temporary. All believers are to be *"where I am,"* in heaven, in the glory into which Jesus is returning *"that they may behold My glory which You have given Me."* Believers are to see Jesus in all the wonders of glory with unspeakable delight. This implies our being in heaven and in the presence of Jesus, glorified and beholding the blessedness of the glory of the exalted Redeemer. The prayer of Jesus reaches back into all eternity. *"Before the foundation of the world"* God loved Him, and at the same time reaches forward to all eternity and the blessedness we shall share in glory with Him forever. The love of God is dated in timeless eternity.

The close of Jesus' prayer is with a word of complete confidence in the righteousness of the Father. He presents all the facts before His righteous Father. The love of Jesus is now to fill the disciples as a blessed treasure. The Father and the Son would dwell in the hearts of the disciples. Jesus expresses assurance that the Father will hear Him.

Daily Bible Study Questions for Group Discussion

Note: Read notes and scripture references before answering the questions. Some questions are for those more advanced in Bible study. Try to answer all questions but don't be discouraged if some seem a little hard. Unless otherwise instructed, use Bible only in answering questions.

FIRST DAY: Read notes on Lesson #26.

1. Make a list of incidents that most impress you in the ministry of Jesus to this point in our study of the book of John.

2. In either the notes or lecture, what did you find most interesting in the prayer of Jesus? **(John 17)**

3. What are some of the most helpful thoughts as far as our responsibility to the Word of God?

SECOND DAY: Read John 18:1-3.

4. What alternative could Jesus have planned if He had wanted to avoid a confrontation with Judas, knowing that Judas planned to betray Him?

5. What important facts are given in the first few verses of **John 18** which help set the stage for Jesus' arrest?

6. In reading **John 12:19** and considering it with **John 18:3**, why do you think so many would need to be involved in taking one man, with eleven nonviolent followers?

THIRD DAY: Read John 18:4-11.

    7.   What makes the scene at the garden unusual as compared to a normal arrest?

    8.   (a) What is indicated by the words *they drew back and fell to the ground*?

            (b) What indication is there of the continuing protective love Jesus had for His disciples?

    9.   Peter's love neither listened nor obeyed Christ but acted on its own. What had Peter so soon forgotten in his protective act for Jesus which the Master rebuked?

10. What is meant by *"the cup which My Father has given Me?"*

FOURTH DAY: Read John 18:12-27.

11. To what two preliminary trials was Jesus subjected before He went before Pilate? What is significant about these trials, since Jewish law forbade a trial to be held during the night?

12. Hate breeds hatred. What indignity did Jesus suffer while on trial before the high priest?

13. When Jesus was questioned by the high priest as to His disciples and His doctrine, what four statements did He make?

14. What was Jesus' recommendation to the high priest, which to be corrected for breach of procedure must have irritated the religious leader?

FIFTH AND SIXTH DAYS: Read John 18:12-27 and John 18:28-40.

15. In what way did Peter fulfill the statement Jesus made regarding him in **John 13:38**?

16. What gross inconsistency or hypocrisy in the action of the Jews is in **John 18:28**?

17. What do you find most interesting about the trial of Jesus before Pilate?

18. What indication is there that Pilate was a weak ruler who did not have the courage to stand for justice?

19. Make a list of the questions Pilate asked Jesus.

20. How would you evaluate the trial of Jesus?

21. In Pilate's proposition to the Jews, what statement would further anger them?

Notes

Notes

The Trial of Jesus
John 18-20

Introduction

The crucifixion and the resurrection form the climax of the Book of John. John, the writer of the Gospel, was an eyewitness during the days of the ministry of Christ and is an eyewitness to the very end, including the trial, crucifixion, resurrection and ascension of Jesus. For the purpose of this gospel, he selects the material from the life of Christ that is in accord with his particular plan and purpose in writing. He is not writing a complete narrative. His purpose is *"That you may believe that Jesus is the Christ, the Son of God, and that believing you may have life in His name."* He carries this theme from the first chapter to the last. Events included in other gospels are omitted in John, sometimes on the supposition that the facts are already known to us. He includes much that is not included in the synoptic gospels, additional information that completes the narrative.

I.   The Arrest of Jesus - Events at the Garden (John 18:1-12)
A. Jesus and His Disciples (John 18:1)

In all probability, Jesus did not leave the upper room until after the discourses and the prayer with the eleven disciples. After leaving the room Jesus and His disciples went out of the city to a garden, which John says was the garden *"over the Brook Kidron,"* which lies between the walled city and the Mount of Olives toward the East. The direction of the garden from the city is mentioned only by John and is not included in the synoptic gospels. This was a dry brook except for a little water in the winter season. The garden mentioned is without doubt the Garden of Gethsemane. Gethsemane means "oil-press" which indicates it was a grove of olive trees. It was into this garden that Jesus and His disciples entered.

B. Judas (John 18:2-3)

Judas, as one of the disciples, had spent the nights here in the garden with them so He knew where Jesus was most likely to be. The record of the agony Jesus suffered in this garden is found in the other gospels. In all probability, Jesus and His disciples had spent Tuesday and Wednesday nights in Gethsemane. It was no doubt easy for Judas to lead a detachment of soldiers and a squad of temple-guards to the place where Jesus was. The detachment of so many soldiers and guards indicates that perhaps there was fear of a confrontation in favor of Jesus. At least they were prepared if such a situation arose. It would have been easy for Jesus to frustrate the plans of Judas had He avoided Gethsemane and gone to another place for the night. Judas and his company of civil, government and religious authorities came to the garden with lanterns, torches and weapons, and a determination to capture their victim. They had sealed the situation against any chance of His escape. Had Jesus chosen to use His power, they would have been His captives rather than He theirs. But Jesus voluntarily surrendered to His enemies.

C. Jesus Faced His Enemies (John 18:4-9)

After Judas had identified Jesus, (the synoptics tell us he identified Him with a kiss), he stepped back and joined the company of the armed crowd. John wants us to know that Jesus acted in full consciousness of all that awaited Him: *"Jesus therefore, knowing all things that would come upon Him, went forward and said to them, 'Whom are you seeking?'"* Jesus immediately took the situation out of the hand of Judas into His own. We can imagine that Jesus met the captors with authority and with the voice that had constrained the devil himself, the demons of the possessed and even death itself. To the question of, *"Whom are you seeking?"* came the response, *"Jesus of Nazareth,"* and Jesus said, *"I am He."* Jesus had come to deliver Himself into their hands. Two things may have been the reason for the apparent frustration of the armed mob: the challenge of the unexpected question of Jesus and the note of authority demanding an answer. It would be inconceivable that one would deliberately, by His own volition, deliver himself into the hands of His captors. Jesus Himself lays down His life and no man takes it from Him.

At Jesus' unexpected declaration, the crowd stumbled back and fell to the ground. John reports tragically, *"And Judas, who betrayed Him, also stood with them."* and shared in the miracle of the power of Christ's words. Judas stood among those with whom he belonged at this time. He had experienced the blessings and privileges of being with Jesus and the other disciples but had made a choice to separate from them in worldly pursuit. John brings in the traitor because he wants to remind his readers of the terrible act of betrayal and being so bold as to identify Christ to the armed mob. At this time, something more than a psychological and natural effect happened upon the crowd. The divine power of Christ was displayed and this indicated to both the Jews and also to the disciples that if the Lord did not voluntarily intend to give Himself unto death, He would have been able to protect Himself and to overcome His enemies, not needing the help of others.

The enemies of Jesus had stated twice that their purpose for coming was to take Him. Jesus said, *"Therefore, if you seek Me, let these go their way."* In this critical moment, Jesus so guarded His disciples that He did not lose one of them. Jesus had included the protection of His disciples in His prayer and God honored this. Potentially the lives of the disciples could have been in grave danger also, but the disciples, as we are told, left Jesus after He had been bound and taken away. This was part of *"the little while"* that we studied in a previous lesson. Jesus kept His disciples out of the hands of those who were arresting Him, even though Peter disregarded the warnings of Jesus and ignored the protection Jesus promised them.

D. Peter's Courage and Presumptuous Act (John 18:10 11)

Knowing a little of Peter's characteristics, it is not surprising that he carried a sword. Jesus had already declared His readiness to submit to arrest and had asked for the release of the disciples. At this point there must have been a move to lay hands on Jesus to bind Him. Peter asked no questions but drew his sword and cut off the ear of the high priest's servant.

Whether or not Peter intended to inflict more extensive bodily injury to this one with the mob we cannot say. Jesus immediately intervenes. *"Put your sword into the sheath."* Peter may have thought, after observing the falling over of the mobs, that with swords and the power of Christ they might defeat this whole plan of the capture of Jesus, and He and the disciples would be the victors. The arm of flesh is always short in fighting spiritual battles. Peter had told Jesus he was ready to lay down his life for his Master. Now he wanted to make good his word. However, this was a poor show of love because it was expressed with violence which is never a part of love. Peter had so soon forgotten the discourses of Jesus that He intended to lay down His life and by death go to His Father. Here in the garden Jesus had voluntarily offered Himself to His captors.

John does not report the miracle of Jesus healing the ear of Malchus. Jesus forbids such rash deeds from His followers. By healing the damages inflicted by Peter, Jesus protected him from the serious consequences which could have followed such an act. Jesus further rebuked Peter, for his act was against the plan of God and the will of Jesus. *"Shall I not drink the cup which My Father has given Me?"*

Shall Jesus, who has come for the very purpose of doing His Father's will, now evade that will and refuse the cup? The drinking of the cup on the part of Jesus was not a mere incidental part of the Father's will, but the supreme part of that will. *"And being found in appearance as a man, He humbled Himself and became obedient to the point of death, even the death of the cross."* (Philippians 2:8). The cup was filled with bitterness.

II. The Trials of Jesus before Religious Authorities and the Denial of Peter (John 18:12-27)

A. Jesus before Annas (John 18:12-23)

After being taken from the garden, Jesus was taken during the night to Annas for questioning. Annas most likely lived in the house of Caiaphas, who was his son-in-law and acting high priest at the time of Jesus' arrest, trial and crucifixion. Annas was of the same mind as his son-in-law regarding Jesus. The news spread about the capture of Jesus and a quorum of the High Court of the Sanhedrin would convene for the trial of Jesus. The legal restrictions forbidding trials at night were set aside, and the Sanhedrin was summoned. These men who deliberately plotted the murder of Jesus would not be bothered by a technicality of legal procedure when at last they had hold of their victim. The reason Jesus was first brought to Annas was personal, not official. It was not Annas who issued the order to arrest Jesus. He was not the real high priest. The questioning before Annas probably took place while they were waiting for the convocation of the Sanhedrin, of which Caiaphas would preside.

When the soldiers closed in to take Jesus in the garden, all the disciples fled. Later, two of the disciples began to follow at a safe distance. Love drew them to follow; fear kept them at a distance. The unnamed disciple is John, himself. Throughout the gospel, when referring to himself, he omits his name. It was through John's influence that Peter could enter the high priest's court where Peter sadly failed in his courage to stand up and identify himself with the one accused, his Lord and Master. It has been suggested that John's knowledge of those at the court was because he was related in some way to the high priest. This, however, is total speculation. There does seem to be some reason why he apparently had privileges for the high priest's court and for the palace. John tells us that the very maid who let Peter into the court exposed his identity. She asked, *"You are not also one of this Man's disciples, are you?"* Peter is compelled to reply, and he denies his discipleship. All his heroic motivations and the courage he had previously displayed are gone. Here he stands a coward, unable to confess his Lord. The suddenness of his exposure before the crowd caused him to lie about his identity.

B. The Trial of Jesus before Caiaphas, the High Priest (John 18:19-24)

Christ's examination before the high priest covered two points: one concerning His disciples and the other concerning His teachings or doctrine. The high priest acted as if he did not know what Jesus taught, as if he had not deemed it worthwhile to acquaint himself with the teaching of this inferior man. The questions are full of hostile intent. He was searching for something that may be used for condemning Him to death. The course pursued by the high priest was

wrong. Therefore Jesus points this out to him and indicates what the right procedure should be. Jesus answers only that which has to do with His doctrine, for only if the doctrine of Jesus were false would it be wrong for Him to win disciples. Jesus had not spread His doctrine secretly, but had taught in the most public and proper way. His teaching had been addressed to the world, not to the Jewish people or the nation Israel.

The question Jesus asked the high priest was based on his reason or intent for asking these questions of Jesus. Again the intent is to get Jesus to say something that will condemn Himself. Jesus suggested that the hearers are the ones who should be called in to testify if the high priest really wanted to serve justice and know the truth. They were the ones to prove any false teaching of Jesus.

C. Jesus Insulted by an Officer of the Court (John 18:22)

Quick to see the difficulty of the high priest, the guard took the opportunity to hit Jesus a violent blow in the face. The blow with the hand was considered especially shameful. He probably thought this would please the high priest. The guard justifies his action by indicating that Jesus had acted discourteously and lacked respect. The answer Jesus gave the guard was with calmness and He exposed the falseness of it in the same manner in which He had exposed the high priest's examination. Jesus lays bare the ugly motive prompting the man's vicious blow. John tells us that following the questioning of Annas, Jesus was sent to Caiaphas and the Sanhedrin for trial.

D. Second and Third Denials of Peter (John 18:25-27)

The Gospel of John tends to be quite brief in recording the three denials of Peter. The first denial is recorded in 18:15-18 and the second and third denials in verses 25-27. He records the facts: Peter denied His Lord three times, and *"immediately a rooster crowed."* The denial of Peter is a tragic story, and the synoptic gospels record the agony of Peter's heart when He remembered what Jesus had told him. Here is a strong, courageous man weeping his heart out, so to speak, because Peter really loved the Lord, but the flesh was found to be weak without the support of a loving Shepherd. These were crucial dark hours for both the disciples and for Jesus.

III. The Roman Trial - Jesus before Pilate (John 18:28-40)

Following the trial before the Sanhedrin, Jesus was taken to the judgment hall of Pilate, where He was placed in the hands of the Roman court to be tried by the Roman governor. Jesus was taken to Pilate to secure the execution of the death sentence which the Sanhedrin had passed. The trial took place between six and seven o'clock in the morning. Jesus arrived at the judgment court under heavy guard, probably to prevent an attempt by friends of Jesus, who had come to Jerusalem for the Passover, from trying to rescue Him. The Jews used all their resources to gain their end. Fearing that they would become defiled, they would not enter the court of the Gentiles, for this would exclude them from eating the Passover. Here we see men who were scrupulous about contracting defilement that would prevent them from keeping the feast, but openly determined in an act of judicial murder.

The Roman court proceedings were conducted in an open and public manner. Pilate opens the court. He takes his seat in the judge's chair and begins the Roman trial. Pilate assumes that the Sanhedrin have come with one or more charges against Jesus and he demands to hear their accusations. This was the last thing that they wanted to hear. They did not want a retrial of Jesus under a Roman judge but acceptance of the verdict they had passed to execute Jesus. The enemies of Jesus were in a difficult position, so they did not answer Pilate's question in a direct manner but took refuge in generalities. *"What accusation do you bring against this Man?"* For Jesus to be a "malefactor" or "evil-doer" meant one thing to Pilate, that Jesus had committed a great crime against Roman law. No such accusations had been placed against Jesus. The death penalty had been pronounced against Him for calling Himself the Son of God, and they called this blasphemy. They had not even attempted to prove that Jesus was not the Son of God. The

Romans would have nothing to do with a Jewish religious matter unrelated to Roman law. This is why they had to lie about the charges brought against Jesus. Pilate is ready to hear the case as a Roman judge, but that would include the accusations brought against Jesus. Otherwise, if this was not what the Jews wanted, Pilate would turn the case back to the Sanhedrin to try the man according to their law.

All that the Jews could inflict was expulsion from the synagogue and scourging with rods up to a certain number of blows. In John 18:31, the Jews revealed their purpose in coming to Pilate. Jesus was to be put to death according to their court, and their court was without legal power to execute this sentence without the Roman government's stamp of approval. Like the death itself, the manner and form of the death of Jesus was under God's control. Jesus was not to suffer death by stoning, crushing and mutilation, but by crucifixion.

Jesus was turned over to the Roman governor for questioning. Pilate selected the main charge made against Jesus, His claim to be Christ, *"a king."* This had political inferences, as reference to a king meant claiming secular power. The implications was that Jesus wanted to be head of a Jewish rebellion against the authority of the Roman government. Jesus had repudiated this. At His entry into Jerusalem, He was hailed *"the King of Israel."* In this Roman trial, John brings out the supreme royalty of Jesus. As Pilate inquires into what Jesus had done, he soon comes to the conclusion that Jesus was innocent. To come to this conclusion and to act upon that decision were two different things. He had to face a blood-thirsty mob with that decision, and in this Pilate avoided conviction and justice. He attempted to have Jesus released on the basis of a custom of releasing a prisoner at this feast time, but the mob demanded the release of a robber instead. Pilate's placing Jesus alongside a convicted criminal, as potential for release by choice of the people, was unjust and weak.

Daily Bible Study Questions for Group Discussion

Note: Read notes and scripture references before answering the questions. Some questions are for those more advanced in Bible study. Try to answer all questions but don't be discouraged if some seem a little hard. Unless otherwise instructed, use Bible only in answering questions.

FIRST DAY: Read notes on Lesson #27.

    1. List as many physical indignities and injustices to Jesus that you can find in **John 18**.

    2. How would you evaluate the trial of Jesus before Pilate? What are Pilate's weak points? What are his strong points as a Roman ruler in handling the case of Jesus?

    3. Rather than have Jesus tried before the Roman governor, what did the Jews really expect Pilate to do?

SECOND DAY: Read John 19.

    4. What great inconsistency do we find in the first five verses of **John 19**?

5. Instead of having the effect Pilate had hoped, what incredible effect did the scourging, the purple robe and the crown of thorns have on the Jews?

6. In trying to comprehend the Jewish religious leaders' hatred of Jesus, was another issue involved that was not brought out at the trial? (Consider previous lessons.)

7. (a) What seems so ridiculous about the vacillation between Jewish law and Roman law?

   (b) What truth finally comes out as the real reason for wanting Jesus killed?

THIRD DAY: Read John 19:8-13.

8. What is indicated by the phrase in **verse 8**, following the reason given by the Jews for wanting to kill Jesus, that Pilate *"was the more afraid?"*

9. What are some indications that Pilate might have realized too late he had made a mistake in promising to turn Jesus over to the Jews for His crucifixion?

10. In **verse 11**, to whom was Jesus referring as having the greater sin? Why?

11. (a) Considering the political threats of the Jewish people to Pilate on this tragic day, do you feel this influenced Pilate as to his final decision to crucify Jesus?

    (b) Who would really reap the consequences of the action on that day?

FOURTH DAY: Continue reading John 19.

12. What demand of the Jewish religious leaders did Pilate refuse?

13. List as many prophecies as you can find in this chapter that were fulfilled at the crucifixion. From your center references, write the Old Testament reference and content of each.

14. What are the words recorded in this chapter that are so significant as to Jesus' obedience in fulfilling, to the end, God's plan for our redemption?

FIFTH DAY:

15. After the display of the worst in human characters, what acts of love and devotion were shown for the One who loved and gave His all?

16. What interesting similarity do you find in the text about Joseph and Nicodemus?

17. As we Christians rejoice in eternal life in Jesus Christ, what should we always remember?

SIXTH DAY:

18. There are certainly spiritual reactions following a study on the trial and crucifixion of Jesus. If you can, share with your discussion group what this has meant to you.

19. Think about those involved with the account of the crucifixion: the religious leaders, Pilate, the bystanders, the soldiers, Jesus' mother, the two other Mary's, Joseph and Nicodemus. Make a list of the various attitudes expressed.

20. (a) What was most meaningful to you from this lesson on **Chapter 19**?

(b) What was the most challenging question?

Notes

The Crucifixion and Burial of Jesus
John 19

Introduction

In this and in the previous chapter, Pilate was dealing with a system of religion in which its leaders pretended to have an exclusive possession of truth. Seeing the hollowness of the clammering mob, he seemingly tended to appease rather than oppose. His question, *"What is truth?"* is sarcasm and a cry from the depths of a soul agonizing for evidence. God's truth is bypassed by a superficial world searching for reality. The religious leaders of that day were poor examples of truth. How important it is today for Christians to know truth and abide by the Word of Truth, that a world lost in its superficiality will somehow be guided to truth as it is in Jesus Christ.

I. Pilate's Final Attempt to Release Jesus (John 19:1-16)

The Gospel of John gives the full account of Pilate's examination of Jesus. The scene constantly changes because Pilate goes outside of the judgment hall to confer with the Jews who refuse to enter a Gentile establishment. Pilate's attempt to free Jesus by way of complying with the custom of releasing a prisoner at the feast had failed. He then ordered Jesus to be scourged and permitted his soldiers to stage mockery of this King of the Jews.

A. Scourging and Mocking Jesus (John 19:1-6)

The scourging of Jesus by Pilate may have been a way of appealing to the pity of the Jews and thus avoiding the sentence of crucifixion. None of the gospels give a description of the scourging; therefore it is necessary to depend on Jewish historians for this information. The prisoner was stripped of his clothing and the body was bent forward across a low pillar so that the back was stretched and exposed to the blows. To hold the body in position, the victim's hands

must have been tied to rings in the floor or at the base of the pillar in front and the feet to the rings behind. The Romans did not use rods as the Jews did. They used short-handled whips, each provided with leather lashes which were ugly acorn-shaped pieces of lead or lumps of bone fastened to the end of each short lash. The strokes were laid on with full force and when the executioners tired, the officers shouted demands to use more force. The effect was horrible. The skin and the flesh of the back were lashed to the bone, and where the ends of the lashes struck, deep, bloody holes were torn. The scourging could have been the reason that Jesus died after being on the cross only six hours. Many prisoners died after such a scourging. Following the scourging, they dressed Jesus as a king, improvising a crown for Him made out of thorn-bearing twigs. This was to make this king look ridiculous and to do this with cruelty by forcing the crown with its lacerating thorns onto His head. No doubt, this was considered by the soldiers to be the perfect joke. Little trickles of blood would run down the victim's face, marking the hideousness of cruelty. The robe resembled the royal purple robe of kings. The soldiers staged a mock royal reception by saying, *"Hail, King of the Jews."* This was Pilate's weak insult to the Jews, whom he despised. Pilate had Jesus scourged and mocked in order to effect His release, and when this failed He gave the order to crucify Him. Pilate put on display the bruised and bleeding figure of Jesus to convince the Jews that he found no fault in Him. They all saw what Pilate wanted them to see and he said, *"Behold the Man."* Pilate himself had made Jesus this object of pity. He had had Jesus scourged and mocked. One word from Pilate would have prevented the tortuous cruelty afflicted on Jesus. Pilate's pity came too late. No one with any feeling for a fellow human being would have permitted such an outrage. Since he had failed before, he tried once more to win out with his pride. He was determined not to let these Jews dictate his verdict.

It seemed a battle of his will against the will of the Jews, and Jesus was in between. The scourging and the mockery were only means to gain his end to save his pride against the Jews. This act was a defeat for Pilate, and the Jews saw that he lacked the courage to force the issue against them. Pilate should have had the courage to release Jesus when he stated his innocence, *"I find no fault in Him."*

B. Pilate's Final Decision
(John 19:6-19)

The Jews were more determined than ever to have Jesus put to death, and when they saw Him, *"They cried out, crucify Him, crucify Him!"* Pilate said unto them, *"You take Him and crucify Him, for I find no fault in Him."* If they were determined to have Jesus crucified, let them take Him themselves and have Him crucified. The Jews' method of execution was not crucifixion, but by stoning. They did not have the authority to crucify a man. The governor was the only one who held this power. The order was ironic. They knew what Pilate meant and made no move to take Jesus and to crucify Him. Pilate, at this point, should have ordered the soldiers to clear the court and all would have been over, but he was afraid of the Jews, yet his Roman pride did not want to bow to their demands.

In the three verdicts Pilate gave, the one the Jewish leaders wanted was not among them. He told them that he found nothing with which to charge Jesus according to Roman law. As a result, the Jews finally admitted to Pilate that they wanted the authority of their own law, which superseded the Roman law. According to their law, Jesus ought to die because He had committed a capital offense. All they wanted Pilate to do was to seal the verdict they had already made by ordering the execution of Jesus. Jesus ought to die because He had made Himself God's Son. This is the first time for them to expose to Pilate the real crime of which they accused Jesus. It was strictly a religious issue, which to Pilate was no reason at all. Their trumped-up charges were false that Jesus had proclaimed Himself a secular king. He had declared Himself *"God's Son."* It is very interesting to note that at the Jewish trial and also at the Roman trial of Jesus, He was condemned to death, not on false charges but on the basis of His divine Sonship. The Jews claimed He made Himself God's Son, and in truth He was God's Son. For this He was condemned.

When he heard that Jesus had made Himself God's Son, Pilate was gripped with fear. This strange man whom Pilate had dressed up as a mock king made Himself *"God's Son."* What if it were true? Under the moment of fear, Pilate ordered that Jesus be taken back to the Praetorium for further questioning. Pilate asked, *"Where are You from?"* Jesus gave no answer. He had already given Pilate the answer and Pilate replied, *"What is truth?"* Jesus had told Pilate, *"For this cause I was born, and for this cause I have come into the world, that I should bear witness to the truth."* (John 18:37). Jesus was very much aware of the power of the man in whose presence He now stood. Pilate really was like an unstable reed tossed by every wind. Jesus said to him, *"You could have no power at all against Me unless it had been given you from above. Therefore the one who delivered Me to you has the greater sin."* This must have shattered the pride of Pilate, but Jesus meant what He said. Jesus answered Pilate as He did that he might think about his office of governor as being under God with a sense of responsibility to God. No ruler had the power to pass on whether Jesus should live or die. Jesus alone had the power to lay down His life or refuse to lay it down. It was not Pilate who held Jesus in his power, but a higher power held Pilate. So it was from the lips of Jesus that Pilate heard His sentence. Pilate tried to release Jesus following their conversation. When Pilate went again before the Jews, they threatened to expose his misdeeds to Caesar. Both Pilate and the Jews were very much aware of the suspicious and jealous character of the Emperor, who never hesitated to sacrifice an official whose loyalty was questionable. The very thought that Caesar might get word about what the Jews were now saying threatened Pilate. He either sacrificed Jesus or himself. Pilate now ordered Jesus to be brought before the people and sat down on the judgment seat to give sentence. The fateful moment had come for the final judicial act.

John says *"it was the Preparation Day of the Passover,"* which means it was the Friday of the Passover. All was being prepared for the Sabbath. The law provided complete rest from work on the Sabbath; all preparation of food had to be made on the previous day. John was trying to fix the day of the week on which Jesus died and also the day on which He arose. The death of Jesus occured on

Friday and the resurrection on Sunday. For this reason, the church has selected Sunday for its weekly day of worship.

Pilate said to the mob, *"Behold your King."* The Jews retorted, *"Away with Him, away with Him."* It seems that Pilate aggravated the Jews to the very end. The high priests answered, *"We have no king but Caesar."* These religious leaders of the nation were not content to disown Jesus alone, they disowned any king of their own and pledged themselves to the pagan Caesar. They demonstrated that they deserved no other king. Pilate delivered Jesus to the high priest to be crucified. It was Pilate's soldiers who were to crucify Jesus for the Jews; they made sure the sentence was carried out. Pilate's name is held in ill repute to this day.

II. Jesus Crucified, Dead and Buried (John 19:17-42)
A. The Crucifixion (John 19:17-22)

"So they took Jesus and led Him away." John wants us to see that these are Jewish acts although carried out by the Roman soldiers at Pilate's command. Immediately after Jesus was sentenced, He was led to the place of crucifixion. There was no delay and the law did not require it. Jesus, as the condemned One, would carry His own cross. The place of the crucifixion was Golgotha. John records the actual crucifixion in few words. The agony of crucifixion needs no description. Two malefactors were crucified with Jesus, one on each side with Jesus in the middle.

The superscription *"Jesus of Nazareth the King of the Jews"* was placed on the cross. Pilate insisted on having Jesus crucified as *"King of the Jews."* The title names no crime; it only records a most significant title. It was written in three languages: Hebrew, Greek and Latin, so all the world would know the great title of Jesus. The high priest tried to have the title changed, but Pilate said, *"What I have written, I have written."*

B. The Parting of the Garments (John 19:23-24)

Four soldiers were assigned to crucify Jesus although there were many others present because of the great crowd. *"Then the soldiers, when they had crucified Jesus, took His garments and made four parts, to each soldier a part, and also the tunic.*

Now the tunic was without seam, woven from the top in one piece." It is believed that the four equal parts would have consisted of His robe, girdle, sandals and headcovering. The coat or tunic John puts into a class by itself. This garment was seamless and was probably worn as an outer garment. It was likely the fifth piece of wearing apparel worn by Jesus and this coat was the most valuable. It was for this garment that the soldiers cast lots, thus fulfilling an Old Testament prophecy (Psalm 22:18), *"They divide My garments among them, And for My clothing they cast lots."* Little did these soldiers realize, pagan as they were, that their act of casting lots for the garment of Jesus was a fulfillment of divine prophecy.

C. Jesus Provides for His Mother (John 19:25-27)

Jesus spoke seven words from the cross. The first four have to do with earthly obligations and the last three regarding His affairs with God. Three women stood by the cross and John was standing with them. This could have been following the withdrawal of the soldiers and they were close enough to hear any last word Jesus might utter. Even in His bitter anguish, Jesus thought of His mother. He saw her and the disciple *"Whom He loved"* (John never gives his own name in the gospel). Jesus said to His mother, *"Woman, behold your son."* To John He said, *"Behold thy mother."* Nothing more tender and touching is found in the gospel account than this love of Jesus for His mother. John took Mary to the home where he, his mother and his brother lived in Jerusalem. When John left Jerusalem to minister in another area, he took the mother of Jesus with him. One tradition says that Mary died and was buried in Ephesus, where John later ministered. How long she lived and where she died is not given in Scripture.

D. The Death of Jesus (John 19:28-30)

Three hours passed following Jesus' words to Mary and to John on the cross. The last act of Jesus consisted of the agony during the three hours of darkness and the guilt of the world's sin was put upon Him, and God Himself had to turn His face from Him. When that was over, Jesus had completed His earthly work. Nothing more was needed. The Scripture was fulfilled, a long, great work completed. Death is included in the finished work of Christ: *"I thirst"* is a request for a drink and very probably that His lips and throat might be moistened for the last saying of Jesus that was so important. The vinegar and the sponge were there to be used for the very purpose for which they were now used....to moisten the lips of the dying. Men who were crucified cried for drink and the executioners used a sponge of vinegar on a short rod to give them enough to moisten their lips. After Jesus received the vinegar He said, *"It is finished."* Matthew and Mark gospels record that Jesus cried with a loud voice. Jesus gave up His spirit into His Father's hands. He returned to the Father after doing the Father's will. The passion and death of Jesus Christ was for us, for you and me. The Lamb of God has made His great sacrifice for the world. Our great Substitute has paid the price of ransom. Others will teach and preach and the work of Jesus will go forth, but the redemptive shedding of His blood, done once for all, is finished and stands as finished forever. Jesus bowed His head and gave up His Spirit, giving Himself unto death for us. Jesus Himself tells us His spirit went into His Father's hands, and this is in heaven. John terms it that He returned to the glory which the Son had with the Father from eternity (John 17:5). The day Jesus died was the darkest day in all of human history and yet it is the brightest, too, for it is through this sacrifice of Jesus on the cross that we have eternal life. Today He lives and makes intercession for us before the throne of the Father.

E. The Piercing of Jesus' Side
(John 19:31-37)

Following the death of Jesus, it was necessary for the Jews to remove the body from the cross before sundown. Jesus died about three o'clock. The Jews had seemingly won the battle; now their thoughts turn to preparing for the Sabbath day. The Jews requested Pilate to have the legs broken on the victims so that death would be hastened and all would be completed before the Sabbath began at sundown. The soldiers broke the legs of the two malefactors who were crucified with Christ, but when they saw that Jesus was already dead they pierced His side. A spear was used as this was the most suitable weapon for such a thrust. It is probable that they pierced the left side of Jesus, intending to pierce the heart. John records these last two incidents in the death of Jesus because he certainly was an eyewitness, and both these incidents fulfilled two prophecies concerning Christ:

one, that no bone in His body would be broken and the other that Jesus was pierced. Both were miracles with the circumstances under which Jesus was crucified. Both fulfilled prophecies proved that Jesus was dead and not merely unconscious as some false teachers believe.

John breaks into the narrative, which is unusual, to assure his readers regarding his testimony. He records that "he who has seen has testified, and his testimony is true." His testimony was based on personal vision, on what he had seen, not on what others told him. The purpose for which John writes is stated here and again in John 20:31, *"That you may believe that Jesus is the Christ, the Son of God."*

In verses 36 and 37, the prophecies referred to are in Exodus 12:46 and Numbers 9:12. The second prophecy is found in Zechariah 12:10. *"They will look on Me whom they pierced."* Zechariah says, *"The inhabitants of Jerusalem . . . will mourn for Him as one mourns for his only son, and grieve for Him as one grieves for a firstborn."* The fulfillment of this prophecy is found in Matthew 24:30, "Then the sign of the Son of Man will appear in heaven, and then all the tribes of the earth will mourn, and they will see the Son of Man coming on the clouds of heaven with power and great glory." Revelation 1:7, *"Behold, He is coming with clouds, and every eye will see Him, even they who pierced Him. And all the tribes of the earth will mourn because of Him."*

F. The Burial of Jesus
(John 19:38-42)

Joseph of Arimathaea and Nicodemus were both members of the Sanhedrin; obviously they were opposed to the action of this body. Each was a secret follower of Jesus because of the fear of the Jews and because of their threat of expulsion from the synagogue to anyone who confessed Jesus. Joseph and Nicodemus both showed courage in having part in the burial of Jesus. They both were men of material means and men of influence in the community. Joseph was the one who requested the body of Jesus, that he might carefully and lovingly see that it was buried rather than thrown into a gutter with the two malefactors, the common grave of the criminal. Pilate gave his permission for Joseph to bury Jesus. Perhaps Joseph bought the linen and the Scriptures tell us that Nicodemus bought the spices. They wrapped the body of Jesus with linen and with the spices after the manner of the Jews and buried Him in a sepulchre in a garden close to Golgotha. The other gospels tell us this was the sepulchre or tomb belonging to Joseph. The tomb is described as *"new tomb in which no one had yet been laid."* Tombs were commonly hewn out of rock and closed with a heavy stone. We are told also in the other gospels that the tomb was sealed by the Romans so there would be no possibility of anyone removing the body of Jesus. The Roman soldiers also guarded the tomb.

Daily Bible Study Questions for Group Discussion

Note: Read notes and scripture references before answering the questions. Some questions are for those more advanced in Bible study. Try to answer all questions but don't be discouraged if some seem a little hard. Unless otherwise instructed, use Bible only in answering questions.

FIRST DAY: Read notes on Lesson #28.

1. After studying the trial of Jesus, what comment do you have concerning the character and purpose of the Jewish leaders?

2. What comment do you have about the character and purpose of Pilate?

3. Who did Jesus say had the greater sin, the Jewish leaders or Pilate? Why?

4. What do you find interesting about the men who supervised the burial of Jesus?

5. The Gospel of John contains three references to Nicodemus: **John 3:1-15; John 7:45-52 and John 19:39-42**. What evidence do you find in him of a growing faith?

SECOND DAY: Read John 20:1-10.

6. What indications are there that the disciples did not expect the resurrection of Jesus?

7. What was Mary Magdalene's interpretation of the stone being moved from the entrance of the tomb? What two astonishing facts did she report to Peter and John?

8. What can we learn from conclusions based on suppositions from the report of the woman?

9. How would you evaluate the reaction of two disciples on the basis of what the Scriptures tell us in John?

THIRD DAY: Continue reading John 20:1-10; read John 20:11-18.

10. Besides the empty tomb, what two strong evidences do we have for the resurrection of Jesus Christ?

11. How would these prove that the body of Jesus was not stolen by the enemies of Christ?

12. With what one thing did Mary seem obsessed as she wept at the tomb?

13. What did it take to convince Mary and cause her weeping and her fears to subside?

FOURTH AND FIFTH DAYS: Read John 20:19-23.

14. What indication do we have that the disciples still were not convinced of the resurrection of Jesus?

15. What evidences had they had to this point that Jesus had risen from the dead?

16. What evidence convinced the disciples and restored gladness to them?

17. Besides giving the disciples peace, what other promise did He make good to them at this time?

SIXTH DAY: Read John 20:24-31.

    18. What demands did Thomas make as a criterion for believing?

    19. In what way did Christ fully meet the demands of Thomas?

    20. What does Jesus promise to those who have not had the privilege of seeing Him with the physical eye, but believe because of His Word and the spiritual life we receive from Him?

Notes

The Resurrection of Jesus Christ
John 20

Introduction

In First Corinthians, Paul writes, *"Now if Christ is preached that He has been raised from the dead, how do some among you say that there is no resurrection of the dead? But if there is no resurrection of the dead, then Christ is not risen. And if Christ is not risen, then our preaching is empty and your faith is also empty."* Those who deny the resurrection of Jesus have set themselves against the entire New Testament as well as the Old Testament prophets. If Christ is not risen from the dead we have no Christianity, no faith, no hope and no Christian church, for we have no Christ and no Redeemer.

I. The Empty Tomb - Mary, Peter and John at the Sepulchre (John 20:1-10)

We learn from the other gospels that there were other women besides Mary Magdalene at the tomb of Jesus very early the morning following the Sabbath, which would be Sunday, the first day of the week. John tells us only what one of the women did. Mary Magdalene was the one to run quickly and inform Peter and John about the empty tomb, and Jesus appeared to her as she was weeping in the garden by the tomb.

The women who went to the tomb so early that Sunday morning knew that the stone at the entrance would be a hindrance to their being able to anoint the body of Jesus with the spices they had so lovingly prepared. As they approached the place of burial, they saw that the stone had been taken away and the door of the tomb opened. They came to the conclusion that someone had taken the body of Jesus away to another place. Perhaps the enemies had come and stolen it to dispose of it in a more cruel manner. This conclusion would be natural when you realize how dif-

ficult it would be for one to open the tomb. The door of this tomb was closed by a great circular slab of stone, rolled into a groove in front of the door, fitting tightly against the face of the cliff into which the tomb had been hewn. This being taken away, it would be easy to assume that the grave had been violated. The women were convinced that the body of Jesus had been stolen by the Jews. It was Mary Magdalene who ran for help. Finding Peter and John she exclaimed, *"Because they have taken away my Lord, and I do not know where they have laid Him."* Her words to the disciples were a request for help. Perplexed by Mary's report, they went at once to the tomb. John, probably because he was younger, ran faster than Peter and came first to the tomb. As John looked into the grave, he saw the linen clothes lying undisturbed with the body of Jesus gone. When Peter arrived he immediately went inside the tomb and John followed. This shows the difference between the personalities of John and Peter. Peter saw exactly what John did. The grave clothes were just as they had been wound about the limbs and the body, but Jesus was no longer in them. It would be impossible for one so bound in grave clothes to slip out of them without disturbing them. If the body had been taken by enemies the grave clothes would have been cut or stripped off and left on the floor. Enemies would have taken the body as it was, wrapped in the grave clothes. Both their presence and the fact that they were undisturbed spoke one thing: Jesus was risen from the dead! The napkin that was about Jesus' head lay in a place by itself, neatly folded to indicate it was orderly placed there. The Scriptures say John saw and believed, but Peter's reaction is not recorded. Luke says he went home wondering at what occurred.

Even though Jesus had told them about His passion and resurrection, they did not understand. *"For as yet they did not know the Scripture, that He must rise again from the dead."* This was their problem, for they followed their own feelings rather than believing what Christ had told them before His death. John, as he reflects now on the resurrection, realizes that even the prophecies of the Old Testament should have been a guide to them. The real basis of faith is "the Scripture." The disciples not only had failed to understand the Old Testament Scripture, they had failed to understand the Words of Christ. Their minds were too occupied with themselves, their loss, their future, rather than believing the wonderful promises Jesus gave to them. Jesus said in Matthew 22:29, *"You are mistaken, not knowing the Scriptures nor the power of God."* What God promises He will fulfill.

The disciples did not remove the linen from the grave, but after a while they left the scene of the empty tomb and returned to their homes. Nothing is mentioned of their inner feelings, the perplexity they surely must have felt, but only that each returned to his own home. Fear may have gripped their hearts that the Jews might accuse them of taking the body of Jesus away. Even that is supposition.

II. The Appearances of Jesus
(John 20:11-29)

A. Jesus Appears to Mary Magdalene
(John 20:11-18)

Mary returned to the tomb, no longer looking for help. She stood and wept. She may have been assured by the disciples that no enemy would have taken the body of Jesus. The evidence was against that, but the mystery of the disappearance of the body was still unsolved. In her bitter sorrow, she looked into the tomb and saw two angels sitting where the body of Jesus had been, one at the feet, the other at the head. Their white garments may represent joy and victory, and symbolize the triumph of life over death. These two heavenly witnesses attest to the resurrection of Jesus. The Scriptures do not say why the angels appeared to the women and not to the men, but we may rest assured that God arranged all the circumstances surrounding the resurrection of Jesus.

Had it not been for angels speaking to Mary, she probably would not have recognized them because of her state of mind and deep grief. The angels said to her, *"Woman, why are you weeping?"* She replied, *"Sir, if You have carried Him away, tell me where You have laid Him, and I will take Him away."* Why did Mary weep? Why was she intent on finding the dead body of her Lord? The very thing for which she

wept was vital to her and to all generations for in it enfolded our redemption. The empty tomb, the angels, the empty linen grave clothes — all are witnesses to what Jesus had said to them, that on the third day He would rise again! How often are we like Mary? If only we would remember God and His Word, we would not grieve needlessly where grief need not exist. God wants us to know the fullness of joy by believing His Word. Grief and tears can blind our eyes and our hearts and obscure the blessing He has for us. The dead body of Jesus was the last link that bound her heart to her Lord. Blinded as she was with grief, she did not even recognize Jesus when she first saw Him, that is not until He spoke to her, *"Woman, why are you weeping?"* She, supposing it to be the gardener, repeated her request to know where they had taken the body of her Lord. Jesus had not asked Mary what she was seeking, but *"Whom"* she was seeking. *"What"* would have been the dead body of her Lord. *"Whom"* implies a living person. Mary would be right in seeking one living, but wrong to continue to seek one who is dead. Jesus was there, her living Lord, and could have helped her. She must stop sobbing if she was to see the proof of Jesus' resurrection, to see Jesus Himself.

Mary recognized Jesus when He spoke her name, *"Mary."* Jesus showed Mary that He knew her name. Mary responded to Jesus by calling Him in the Hebrew, *"Rabboni."* Mary, recognizing her Master, fell at His feet to worship Him, clinging to the blessed feet in such a way to assure her that He would not leave. This was the first impulse of her heart to hold whom she had lost. Now He is here, not dead but alive. All her loss she turned into sudden possession. Jesus kindly must say to her, "Do not cling to Me, for I have not yet ascended to My Father; but go to My brethren and say to them, 'I am ascending to My Father and your Father, and to My God and your God.'" This blessed news was not for Mary alone, but for the disciples also. God was Jesus' Father by nature, but He is our Father by grace. He is God's Son, born from all eternity. The message for Mary to give the disciples was, *"and say to them, 'I am ascending to My Father.'"*

Changed from a grief-stricken woman, Mary obeyed the instruction of her Master. She exclaimed, "I have seen the Lord." He had spoken to her and she reported to them the message. We do not know how the disciples received this message.

B. Jesus Appeared to the Disciples (John 20:19-23)

In the evening, on the first day of the week, Jesus appeared to His disciples. The Scriptures tell us they were behind locked doors for fear of the Jews. As the news of an empty tomb became known, probably even greater fear emerged of what action the Jews would take toward the disciples of Jesus. There is much speculation regarding this appearance of Jesus. Those who refuse to recognize the supernatural or miracles try to find other ways of Jesus' entering the room that to them is more rational. All the Scripture records is that Jesus stood in their midst and greeted them with the words, *"Peace to you!"* In His risen and glorified state, time, space, the rock of the tomb, walls and doors no longer limited the risen Christ. It is difficult for us to understand, and perhaps when our bodies eventually enter their heavenly existence, we may know something of these mysteries. After Jesus greeted them, He showed them His hands and His side. The peace Jesus gave to the disciples the night of His betrayal is now renewed. He showed to them the identification marks on His body, indicating the price with which He purchased their peace: His pierced hands, His riven side, the evidence of His death and crucifixion. The disciples were glad when they saw the Lord.

The second gift and assurance of peace forms the basis of the commission Jesus gave to His disciples at this time. They were to be not only possessors of the peace Christ had given them, but were to go forth as His witnesses and messengers to give this gift of peace to a peaceless world: preaching peace by Jesus Christ, for He is our peace. If the disciples were to preach peace, they must be possessors of that peace. The commission of bringing peace and salvation to the world belongs to the entire church. This gospel of peace is its responsibility. It was given to the apostles and then passed on to the early church in the Book of the Acts of the Apostles and it is still in effect for the church today. May God help us in these days to fulfill that responsibility as part of the body of Christ. In the following words Jesus gave to His disciples a gift intended for the entire church. *"And said to them, 'Receive the Holy Spirit.'"*

And He said unto them, Receive ye the Holy Ghost." He enables those He sends, and that enabling is the gift of the Holy Spirit.

C. The Authority of the Commission Given to the Disciples (John 20:23)

"If you forgive the sins of any, they are forgiven them; if you retain the sins of any, they are retained." These words have been the occasion of endless controversy. It is true that the apostles were to be agents through whom Christ was to proclaim the terms of admission to His kingdom. They received authority from Christ to say what sins were to be forgiven and what sins could be retained. It seems that for any man to have power to exclude or admit individuals seeking entrance into the kingdom of God is to leave logic and reason and to establish a kind of government in the church of Christ. That government will never be submitted to by those who live in the liberty in which His truth has made them free. The presence of the Holy Spirit, and no external appointment, is that which gives authority to those who guide the Church of Christ. Because they are inwardly one with Christ, not because they happen to be able to claim an outward connection with Him, they have that authority of Christ's people. It is important to know that the apostles were, by divine inspiration, to declare the privileges and principles of the kingdom of God. No man can forgive sins in the sense of their removal in God's sight. The message and the finished work of Christ of cleansing and forgiveness was accomplished at Calvary. God's Word preached through the power of the Holy Spirit judges a man of sin, of righteousness and judgment to come. After hearing the Word, an individual must respond to that Word. A Christian will know whether or not an individual accepts or rejects, not whether his sins are forgiven or whether he chooses to remain in his sin. It is a serious thing to reject the Word of God.

D. Jesus Appeared to Thomas (John 20:24-29)

The second appearance of Jesus to the disciples was because of Thomas. It seems he was absent at Christ's first appearance because he obstinately refused to believe. He is referred to as doubting Thomas. Unbelief always has been and always will be unreasonable. With all the unanimous testimony of those who had seen the Lord, Thomas still refused to believe. At this point Thomas was more than a doubter; he was an unbeliever. He challenged the evidence the others presented. If he is to believe, he demands to see in Jesus' hands the print of the nails, and to put his finger into these nailprints, and to thrust his hand into His side. Unbelief sets up a criterion of its own and it will have what it demands. So often the unbeliever assumes himself a superior person, looking down on believers whose judgment cannot be trusted. It pretends to obey reason and intelligence alone, but in reality it does the opposite.

One week later, Jesus again appeared to the disciples and this time Thomas was present. The resurrection of Jesus had reunited the disciples after the crucifixion had scattered them. Jesus told Thomas to do exactly what he had insisted upon doing. The divine love of Jesus reached out to Thomas in extending to him the peace and assurance the other disciples already had. The three statements of Jesus correspond exactly to the three Thomas had made. We have a tendency to blame Thomas, but Jesus knew Thomas would have many successors in all ages. By thus dealing with Thomas, meeting him on his own grounds, He is dealing with all doubt and disbelief in His resurrection in all time to come. It is of value to us to see what Jesus did with doubting, disbelieving Thomas. Jesus gave an admonition to Thomas and said, *"Do not be unbelieving, but believing."* Thomas answered and said unto Him, *"My Lord and my God."* Thomas gave Jesus Christ full acceptance of His deity and of the fact of His resurrection. Thomas obeyed the Lord's admonition and showed himself as believing!

Jesus said to him, *"Because you have seen Me, you have believed. Blessed are those who have not seen and yet have believed."*

John's Gospel closes as it begins by proclaiming the deity of Jesus. Jesus accepts the confession of Thomas, for He says, *"You have believed."* Jesus acknowledged that Thomas had come to faith. Christ gave a promise to others, to those who shall believe without first seeing.

III. The Conclusion
(John 20:30-31)

John, in his gospel, selects the material which most adequately satisfies his subject. *"That you may believe that Jesus is the Christ, the Son of God, and that believing you may have life in His name."* John traces through the gospel the Person of the Son of God: His ministry, His passion and His resurrection. The disciples He chose were to be believers, selected and qualified witnesses for the work Christ commissioned them to do. There are many signs and miracles written in the Gospel of John, but he says there were many more. It was not necessary for John to duplicate what others had written. His purpose for writing the gospel is for the practical principle, *"that you may believe."* In Jesus we have the full humanity of the Messiah, and in *"the Son of God"* His deity, joined in the personal union of the incarnation. His ultimate purpose in the gospel is *"that believing you may have life in His name."*

Daily Bible Study Questions for Group Discussion

Note: Read notes and scripture references before answering the questions. Some questions are for those more advanced in Bible study. Try to answer all questions but don't be discouraged if some seem a little hard. Unless otherwise instructed, use Bible only in answering questions.

FIRST DAY: Read notes on Lesson #29.

1. What infallible proofs do we have of the resurrection of Jesus in **John 20**?

2. What would have helped Mary and the other women handle their grief if they had only remembered?

3. The disciples were not as obviously emotional in their reaction to the empty tomb, but do you feel they had basically the same problem?

4. Do you feel the reaction to grief was normal to human nature, and is there something we can learn from this that should be helpful in our experience of grief?

5. What lesson can we learn from Thomas and his demands for proofs or signs before he would believe Jesus was truly alive?

SECOND DAY: Read John 21:1-9.

6. The disciples were in Galilee waiting for further instructions from the Lord. What do you find out about the character of Peter in his saying, *"I am going fishing."* and the disciples response?

7. Not that it was wrong, but what danger could be involved with Peter returning to his old profession?

8. What characteristics are obvious in Peter that made him a good disciple and leader.

THIRD DAY: Read John 21:9-14.

9. Do you feel that it could have been intentional on the part of Jesus not to permit them to be successful on their fishing venture, that He might teach them a lesson? Why?

10. What is highlighted as being part of the miracle in catching so many fish?

11. (a) What do you find in the text to indicate Jesus had fixed breakfast for Himself, yet had enough to feed seven hungry disciples?

   (b) What can we learn from the instructions Jesus gave to His disciples to take care of their catch of fish before they ate breakfast?

FOURTH DAY: Read John 21:15-19; Read John 1:42.

12. What is the significance of the name Jesus used to address Peter in **verse 15**?

13. What is the meaning of the phrase *"more than these"* also found in **verse 15**?

14. What is the significance of Jesus asking Peter three times, *"Do you love Me?"*

FIFTH AND SIXTH DAYS: Read John 21:15-25.

15. Though Peter had failed and denied His Lord, in loving concern Jesus dealt with him and his problem. Jesus commissioned Peter to share in a great ministry. What was he to do?

16. What can we learn from this incident? Apply this to Christian ministry today.

17. What do we learn about the Lord directing each disciple's life and the difference there is from one disciple to another?

18. In essence, what did God promise or predict for Peter as He contrasts young Peter with old Peter?

19. As you think about the complete chapter and Jesus' ministry of further preparing His disciples to undertake the great work that lay ahead of them, what are some basic principles for discipleship?

20. What in the Gospel according to John has been the most meaningful to you?

Notes

The Epilogue
John 21

Introduction

Chapter twenty-one of the Gospel of John deals with incidents in the life of the apostles and is different from records found in the synoptic gospels. The material is considered a supplement to the Gospel. There is no question as to the author being the same as the author of the Gospel itself, whether he penned it with his own hand or dictated it. Since no copies of the Gospel of John have been found that have omitted this chapter, it is definitely considered as part of the Gospel written by John the Apostle immediately following the writing of John, chapters one through twenty. The linguistic evidence is in favor of John having written the chapter.

I. Jesus and the Disciples
(John 21:1-8)
A. The Fishing (John 21:1-4)

The phrase, *"after these things,"* definitely connects this chapter with John 20:26-29. In Mark 14:28, Jesus had told the disciples that after the resurrection He would meet them in Galilee. John, knowing about the directions of Jesus and what happened with the disciples since he was one of them, wrote about the incidents as we have them reported by him in John 21. It mostly has to do with Jesus and Peter, in that Peter had denied the Lord during the time of the trial of Jesus. John felt there was a need for clarification as to Peter's position and commission by Christ.

After the resurrection, Jesus did keep His appointment with the disciples in Galilee at the Sea of Tiberias. What a place this proved to be for Simon Peter! He was a fisherman. After waiting for a time for Jesus to come, Peter decided to go fishing. The story is told in detail. His announcement that he was going fishing was an invitation for the other disciples to join him. It was evening, and since fishing was best at night, they got into the boat to fish while they waited for Christ to meet them. They labored all night and the Scripture tells us *"they caught nothing."* Probably because they were tired and weary, and in the morning haze, they did not recognize Jesus on the shore. He called to ask them if they had something to eat. The answer was negative and Jesus knew they had caught nothing. He told them to cast their nets on the right side of the boat. It is most unusual that one on the shore could give such successful directions. The miracle was instantaneous. There were so many fish they couldn't get them all into the boat. John said to Peter, *"It is the Lord!"* By means of this miracle Jesus had made His presence known to the disciples. Peter put on his garments and left everything, the boat as well as the fish, and went to Jesus. Only an eyewitness could have written about Peter's clothes. John is telling us of the haste with which Peter left the boat. Peter acts on impulse. Impulsive Peter! It is special to know how God takes men with different personalities and uses them to the praise of His glory — like a vessel in a potter's hand, always with rough edges needing to be trimmed, but God has a beautiful way of doing this. He does not choose us for what we are, but for what we will become. It is our willingness to be molded and to be made into His likeness. Richly laden, the disciples went back to shore.

B. The Meal (John 21:9-14)

The miracle of the morning did not end with the catch of fish. Jesus had made a fire and prepared breakfast of a cake and a fish. The fire, the fish and the bread were there also by the miraculous power of Jesus. This certainly would not be enough food for seven hungry fishermen. Jesus instructed them to take care of their catch of fish and then invited them to eat breakfast with Him. Fishermen generally sorted the fish, putting the smaller ones back into the water and keeping the larger ones. This may have been what

Jesus wanted them to do. With the fish properly cared for, they were now ready to eat. The disciples knew this could be none other than their Lord because of the miracles. This was an entirely different approach of Jesus to the disciples and it caused some to question. The miracle of the disciples eating with Jesus is also the multiplication of food. One bread cake and one fish fed the seven disciples. The text does not say Jesus ate with the disciples. It was the third time Jesus appeared to His disciples following the resurrection.

II. Peter and John (John 21:15-23)

A. Peter (John 21:15-19)

John always refers to Peter as Simon Peter. It is interesting that Jesus here addressed Peter as *"Simon, son of Jonah,"* or John. He does not add *"Peter."* Jesus had given to Simon the name, "Peter." He used this old name of the apostle in order to remind him of his natural descent and of all that clung to him in weakness because of it. Peter was impetuous and rough by nature. He had promised faithfulness even to death with Jesus, and then when the test came he had miserably failed and denied His Lord three times. He had shown himself only as Simon, son of John. He had been nothing of what the name "Peter" meant. Following breakfast, as they sat by the fire, Jesus asked Peter questions and Peter answered. The phrase, *"more than these,"* in verse 15 could read "more than these other disciples." Peter's trouble was not with the fact that he had gone fishing, but that he had three times denied the Lord, for whom he had claimed love and loyalty greater and more enduring than that of the other disciples. Jesus wanted Peter to make public confession of this in order to have the hurt completely healed, for Peter's good as well as that of the other disciples. Peter had learned a lot since his fall. He knew his love had been anything but the high love of the true understanding of his Lord and of the sincere purpose of living up to that understanding. How often Jesus had to correct Peter's wrong impulses. *"'Simon, son of Jonah, do you love Me more than these?' He said to Him, 'Yes, Lord; You know that I love You.' He said to him, 'Feed My lambs.'"* In this Peter honors Jesus and places all his trust in Him. *"You know"* His divine knowledge is better to judge what is in my heart than I can. Peter knew Jesus knew what was in the hearts of men. Jesus placed in Peter's loving care His most precious possession, the little ones, the lambs. It seems Jesus places the love and

care of children as a first essential work. The spiritual care of the lambs or little children should be the most delightful work of the shepherd of the flock. Jesus gives it top priority in Peter's commission. Matthew 28:20 says, *"Teaching them to observe all things that I have commanded you."* To feed means to teach the Word of God. To lead children is easy, for they follow. They must grow and become strong and mature and they do not do this on weak supplements. The church's responsibility is to teach and nurture the children with the Word of God.

Jesus said to Peter again, *"Simon, son of Jonah, do you love Me?"* He said to Him, *"Yes, Lord; You know that I love You."* Jesus said to him, *"Feed My sheep."* In this question Jesus omits the comparison of Peter with the other disciples. We must note that the Lord's three questions to Peter are not just repetitions without variations. The question whether Peter loved Jesus more than the other disciples leaves it unquestioned that Peter loves Jesus at least as much as the others and reminds Peter not to put himself above the others. In the second answer he assures the Lord that he loves Him. Jesus then said to Peter, *"Feed My sheep."* Shepherd my sheep. Be doing the work of a shepherd. This means the entire flock and also includes the lambs. This embraces the whole church: the lambs, the sheep and the young sheep. Jesus wanted to impress Peter with the greatness of his responsibility in the commission He gave to him. Peter's love for Christ and his love for the flock is very important to Jesus. Do we take it seriously enough today? The commission Jesus gave to Peter needed all that shepherding implies.

Jesus said to Peter the third time, *"Simon, son of Jonah, do you love Me?"* Peter, grieved or disturbed at the third question, says, *"Lord, You know all things; You know that I love You."* Jesus said to Peter, *"Feed My sheep."* All Peter could do was appeal to the omniscience of Jesus. Peter's hurt was only that Jesus might administer healing for the wound that was so deep from the night of his denial of Jesus. The dealing of Jesus with Peter was a serious reminder of his grave defection, and now Peter had declared his love and devotion for Jesus as often as he had denied Him. His denial was public, so his declaration of his love for Jesus needed to be public, in the presence of other disciples.

After Peter affirmed his love for Jesus, the Lord predicted what kind of death would crown the long faithful life of Peter as an apostle. This is a promise to Peter as well as a prophecy. Peter would have a long, fruitful ministry crowned with a death that Peter would deem worthy to suffer and die for His Lord and Master. The contrast is between the young Peter and the old Peter. Only Jesus could know that Peter would be faithful to his commission as an apostle and would die for the cause of Christ. Peter was executed in the year 64 A.D. The text does not describe the actual mode of Peter's death. Eusebius reports that Peter was crucified by Nero with his head downward. He is the only apostle known to have died by crucifixion.

Peter's life and death shall glorify God. How important it is for each Christian to grow strong into a perfect mind and unto the measure of stature of the fullness of Christ. Jesus said to Peter, *"Follow Me"* (Ephesians 4:13). From beginning to end, Peter's commission involved following Christ. This is a privilege and a responsibility.

B. John (John 21:20-25)

All that Jesus had said to Peter was said beside the fire of coals in the presence of the other disciples. When He had finished talking to Peter, Jesus started to walk away and Peter followed. Turning around and seeing John following also, Peter asked Jesus a question concerning John. Peter said to Jesus, *"But Lord, what about this man?"* Peter had received a prophecy from Jesus regarding his future ministry and death, and Peter's question is an inquiry as to what the Lord may have in store for John, who was Peter's beloved friend and companion. Did the same prospect await John? The question emanates from Peter's love for John. Martyrdom was considered the highest possible honor and distinction any believer might achieve. Peter's question was the reverse of envy, for what Peter asked: "Shall my beloved John have less than is promised me?"

Jesus withholds from Peter what he would really like to know. We should not try to turn what Jesus said into harshness. What Jesus said to Peter was a kindly intimation to leave John's future in the hands of his Lord. God's will regarding John will be revealed at a proper time. Jesus' concern for Peter at this time was that he follow the Lord. The Lord will take care of John. In this statement of Jesus to Peter about John, *"If I will that he remain till I come,"* was spoken conditionally, suppose I will. How many things today are reported on supposition rather than fact either by not reading or hearing correctly. Jesus would let John live as long as He might decide was best. Jesus did not say that John should not die, as was reported.

Verse 23 is of great importance for the genuineness and the authorship of the Gospel of John. John was alive when this chapter was written and was waiting to see what the Lord's will concerning him would be.

Evaluation Review

Note: You may use your Bible and lesson notes.

1. Differentiate between John the Baptist and John the disciple, writer of the Gospel. List as many things as you can easily remember about each.

2. Name the person who spoke each of the following quotations. Give the reference.

    a. *"Rabbi, You are the Son of God! You are the King of Israel!"*

    b. *"We have found Him of whom Moses in the law, and also the prophets, wrote; Jesus of Nazareth, the son of Joseph."*

    c. *"We have found the Messiah" (which is translated, the Christ)."*

    d. *"Behold! The Lamb of God who takes away the sin of the world!"*

3. (a) John Chapter One gives four different ways to find Christ. Describe the method used from the following verses.
    1. **John 1:35-39**

    2. **John :40-42**

    3. **John 1:43**

    4. **John 1:45-46**

    (b) What exciting results were experienced?

4. Give your answer to each of the following questions using a reference from the **3rd Chapter of John**.
    a. What does a person need to do to be saved?

    b. What does a person need to do to be lost?

5. Can you quote from memory the verse in **John 3** that is the one considered to be the most quoted and best loved?

6. Make a list of the seven miracles or signs Jesus did.

7.   **John 6:35** Jesus said: "I am _____ "

       John 8:12 Jesus said: "I am _____ "

       John 10:7 Jesus said: "I am _____ "

       John 10:11 Jesus said: "I am _____ "

       John 11:25 Jesus said: "I am _____ "

       John 14:6 Jesus said: "I am _____ "

       John 15:1 Jesus said: "I am _____ "

8. Thinking about each of the "I am's" of the claims of Christ, write a sentence or phrase to what you think Jesus was teaching in each.

9. Following Jesus' conversation with the woman of Samaria and the result of many coming to Christ, what great verse from the **4th Chapter** is used to emphasize missions?

10. When the Jews purposed a problem between John the Baptist and his ministry with that of Christ, what was John the Baptist's attitude toward Christ? **John 3**.

11. Make a list of several important aspects of Christ's ministry that John expresses in **John 3:31-36**.

12. How did the Samaritan woman try to side track Jesus in their conversation when Jesus exposed her sinful life?

13. What are three concepts of major importance to all human thinking? **(John 8:32)**

14. What did you learn about the difference between a religion and Christianity or the teaching of the Pharisees verses the teaching of Christ? **(Lesson 16, John 9)**

15. It is not by the creed you recite; not by what you wear; not by the hymns you sing; not by the ritual you observe, but by the fact that you love one another. This is the test of discipleship. What verses in **John 13**, give this fact spoken by Jesus?

16. Jesus qualifies His words *"That you also love one another."* with a part of the verse that so often is deleted when we talk about "love". What is it?

17. Considering the answer to question 16 and the ministry of Christ, what are some examples of the *"love of Christ"*?

18. Jesus in teaching the disciples about leaving them gave promise of the Holy Spirit, what does He say that the Holy Spirit will be to us?

19. List the seven things Jesus had done during His earthly ministry as given in the **17th Chapter of John**.

20. In the shameful trial and condemnation of Jesus; whom did Jesus say had the greatest sin?

Something to think about: We rejoice as Christians in eternal life, but let us always remember what it cost. The source of our joy was the pain and suffering of our Lord. Let us faithfully serve Him.

Notes

Appendix:

Maps & Charts

TRINITY CHART
STUDIES IN THE GOSPEL OF JOHN

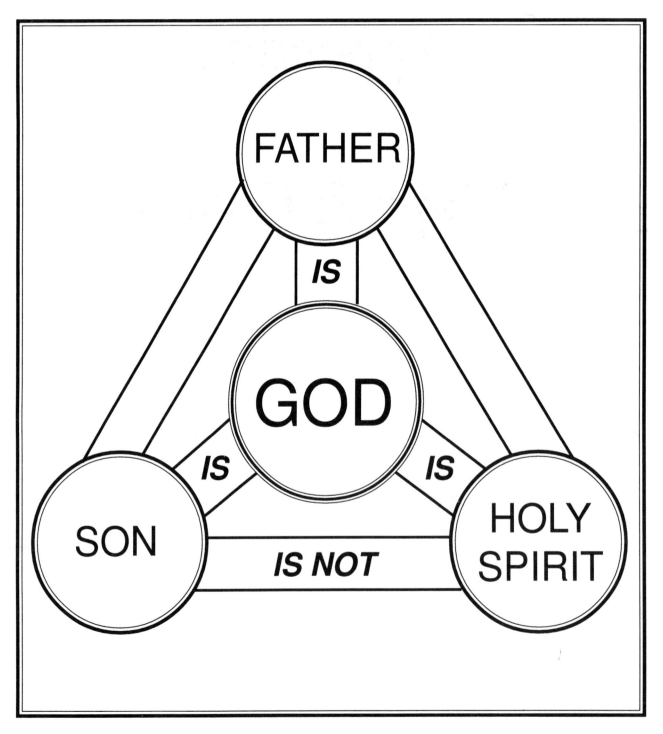